Purposeful Planning for Learning

T0270509

Purposeful Planning for Learning puts the passion and depth back into how teachers plan for learning in the primary classroom. Offering a unique perspective on what constitutes purposeful planning for learning, this book encourages a mindset where planning is integral to, supportive of and informed by learning, including learning that is social, emotional, physical and cognitive.

Written by a variety of teacher educators and primary teachers, this book reconceptualises planning by focusing on different themes such as outdoor learning, assessment, questioning and inclusion, that all influence and inform planning. In each chapter, you can find:

- Voices of teachers and teacher educators
- The unpicking of practice and key terminology
- Vignettes that shed light on classroom life (examples from practice) and
- Opportunities for reflection (points to ponder)

This cross-curricular resource provides aspirational, professional and practical insights into current issues that surround planning. It includes student and experienced qualified teacher insights which will serve as inspiration to support the reader in making real changes in their classroom.

Natasha Serret was a primary teacher and is now a senior lecturer working with the Primary Education team at Nottingham Trent University, where she is the course leader for BA Primary Education. She has collaborated on several research projects, with universities in the UK and across Europe, that have focused on outdoor learning in science, Cognitive Acceleration in Science Education (CASE) and assessment in science education.

Catherine Gripton is a lecturer, author and researcher with many years of experience in primary teacher education. She is an assistant professor in the School of Education at the University of Nottingham and has a special interest in 3–7 education and early childhood mathematics. Catherine was formerly a teacher in Nottingham and Nottinghamshire primary schools.

Purposeful Planning for Learning

Shaping Learning and Teaching in the Primary School

Edited by Natasha Serret and Catherine Gripton

Routledge
Taylor & Francis Group

LONDON AND NEW YORK

First published 2021
by Routledge
2 Park Square, Milton Park, Abingdon, Oxon OX14 4RN

and by Routledge
52 Vanderbilt Avenue, New York, NY 10017

Routledge is an imprint of the Taylor & Francis Group, an informa business

© 2021 selection and editorial matter, Natasha Serret and Catherine Gripton; individual chapters, the contributors

The right of Natasha Serret and Catherine Gripton to be identified as the authors of the editorial material, and of the authors for their individual chapters, has been asserted in accordance with sections 77 and 78 of the Copyright, Designs and Patents Act 1988.

All rights reserved. No part of this book may be reprinted or reproduced or utilised in any form or by any electronic, mechanical, or other means, now known or hereafter invented, including photocopying and recording, or in any information storage or retrieval system, without permission in writing from the publishers.

Trademark notice: Product or corporate names may be trademarks or registered trademarks, and are used only for identification and explanation without intent to infringe.

British Library Cataloguing-in-Publication Data
A catalogue record for this book is available from the British Library

Library of Congress Cataloging-in-Publication Data
Names: Serret, Natasha, editor. | Gripton, Catherine, editor.
Title: Purposeful planning for learning: shaping learning and teaching in the primary school / edited by Natasha Serret and Catherine Gripton.
Description: Abingdon, Oxon; New York, NY: Routledge, 2020. |
Includes bibliographical references and index. |
Identifiers: LCCN 2020014261 | ISBN 9781138593770 (hardback) |
ISBN 9781138593794 (paperback) | ISBN 9780429489266 (ebook)
Subjects: LCSH: Elementary school teaching. | Lesson planning. | Teacher effectiveness.
Classification: LCC LB1555 .P97 2020 | DDC 372.1102—dc23
LC record available at https://lccn.loc.gov/2020014261

ISBN: 978-1-138-59377-0 (hbk)
ISBN: 978-1-138-59379-4 (pbk)
ISBN: 978-0-429-48926-6 (ebk)

Typeset in Bembo and Helvetica Neue
by codeMantra

Dedicated to our wonderful colleague and friend Nicky-Jane Kerr-Gilbert, a passionate teacher.

Contents

Figures

Examples from practice

Tables

Contributors

Natasha Serret was a primary teacher, and is now a senior lecturer working with the Primary Education team at Nottingham Trent University, where she is the course leader for BA Primary Education. She has collaborated on several research projects, with universities in the UK and across Europe, that have focused on outdoor learning in science, Cognitive Acceleration in Science Education (CASE) and assessment in science education.

Catherine Gripton is a lecturer, author and researcher with many years of experience in primary teacher education. She is an assistant professor in the School of Education at the University of Nottingham and has a special interest in 3–7 education and early childhood mathematics. Catherine was formerly a teacher in Nottingham and Nottinghamshire primary schools.

Simon Brown was a primary school teacher for 13 years working with children across the 7–11 age range. He was a maths subject leader in two Leicestershire schools, worked as a local authority primary maths consultant and is currently teaching at Nottingham Trent University in the Primary Education team.

Helen Fielding was a primary school teacher for 20 years working with children across the 5–11 age range. She recently retired from in the Primary Education team at Nottingham Trent University where she specialised in primary mathematics.

Suzanne Gomersall has been involved in Primary Education (PE) for over 20 years, having previously worked as a primary teacher at various Nottinghamshire schools. She is currently a senior lecturer at Nottingham Trent University and has a special interest in Design and Technology and PE. Suzanne is working on her PhD developing a whole school cooking and nutrition programme to tackle childhood obesity.

Elaine Haywood was a primary school teacher for almost 30 years working with children across the primary age range. She worked at Nottingham Trent University in the Primary Education team, specialising in English, and now works mainly with students on school placements.

Sarah Hindmarsh was a primary school teacher in Nottinghamshire before moving to Nottingham Trent University where she had a special interest in outdoor learning as part of the primary science team. She is currently Course Director for Undergraduate Primary Education at Leeds Beckett University.

Susan Hunt was a primary school teacher for 16 years working with children across the 4–7 age range. She has recently retired after seven years working at Nottingham Trent University in the Primary Education team specialising in early years, science and forest school teaching and learning.

Fiona Hunter was a primary school teacher for 11 years working with children across Foundation Stage, KS1 and KS2. Fiona is currently working at Nottingham Trent University in the Primary Education team specialising in inclusion, special educational needs and humanities.

Nicky-Jane Kerr–Gilbert was a primary school teacher for 16 years working with children across the 4–11 age range. She is currently working at Nottingham Trent University in the Primary Education team specialising in primary English.

Laura Malpas was a primary school teacher for over 20 years working with children across the 4–11 age range. She is currently working at Nottingham Trent University in the Primary Education team specialising in primary mathematics.

Vicky McEwan has worked in schools and early years settings for over 20 years working with children across the birth to seven age range. Vicky is currently working at Nottingham Trent University as course leader for postgraduate early years teacher status and on a number of other programmes including Primary Education specialising in early years, leadership and English.

Nick Mills was a primary school teacher for 28 years working in city schools with children across the 5–11 age range. He has recently retired after 11 years at Nottingham Trent University in the Primary Education (PE) team specialising in professional and personal development, PE and behaviour.

Richard Muge was a primary school teacher for 14 years working with children across the 5–11 age range. Richard is currently working at Nottingham Trent University in the Primary Education team specialising in primary geography.

Alison Murphy was a primary school teacher for 9 years working with children across the 4–11 age range. Alison is currently working at Nottingham Trent University in the Primary Education team specialising in science. Alison has been a lecturer for 11 years. Her current research interest lies in outdoor learning and science enquiry.

Clare Orridge was a primary school teacher for 13 years working with children across the 4–11 age range. She is currently working at Nottingham Trent University in the Primary Education team specialising in primary English.

Nick Page was a primary school teacher for 10 years in York then in Hinckley, working with children aged 7–11 years. Nick then worked as an ICT (Information Communication Technology) consultant with Leicestershire School Improvement Services, before moving to Nottingham Trent University where he now works in the Primary Education team specialising in teaching primary computing.

Rob Perkins is a senior leader in a large primary school in Nottingham. He has previously worked in several schools in Nottingham and Nottinghamshire. Rob is particularly interested in primary humanities and assessment.

Eleanor Power was a primary school teacher for 26 years working with children across the 4–11 age range. She is currently working at Nottingham Trent University in the Primary Education team leading primary English and has a special interest in reading for pleasure and developing student teachers as readers.

Liz Ruston was a primary school headteacher for 16 years working with children across the 2–11 age range. Liz is currently working as a senior lecturer at Nottingham Trent University in the Primary Education team specialising in art, and leadership and management.

Steven Sharp has been a teacher for 17 years and has worked in mainstream primary, special, special advisory and behavioural settings with children across the 5-14 age groups. In his previous life he was a soldier, electronics technician and IT manager.

Paul Waring-Thomas is the programme leader for the PGCE Primary Education, primary school direct and apprenticeship courses at Nottingham Trent University. He has been a lecturer at the university for 11 years teaching across the Primary Education Initial Teacher Training courses and specialising in science and professional studies. Prior to that Paul was a primary school teacher working in a Nottingham city school for ten years teaching children across the whole primary age range from 5 to 11 years old and leading science, computing and modern foreign languages at his school.

1

What is planning?

Natasha Serret and Catherine Gripton

If the goal of teaching is children's learning and development, then the learning experiences and our teaching that facilitates this needs to be planned with thought, creativity and professional understanding. Planning is seen as preparation for learning.

The intention of this book is to encourage a mindset where planning is integral to, supportive of and informed by learning. This is learning in its broadest sense so includes social, emotional, physical and cognitive development. Within this conception, planning in this book is recognised as a holistic process. From the thinking that happens on the journey to school and the informal discussions that go on between staff during a school day to the stimuli captured outside of school and the creation of inspiring classroom environments, preparation for learning (or planning) is taking place. In this book, planning is not seen as an individual endeavour. It involves a collaboration with staff, parents, children and the wider school community.

When we set out to write this book, we had in mind an audience of beginning and more experienced teachers and other education professionals from different countries working with children in the 3–11 age range. A key challenge in planning is having a shared understanding of the terminology that is in everyday use in educational settings. In this book, we refer to:

- Your curriculum – as the curriculum used in your setting
- Children – as the children and young people (or pupils) that we teach
- Lesson or activity – a more or less formal learning and teaching moment
- Teacher or practitioner – a facilitator of learning, regardless of their qualification or title
- Student teacher – a beginning facilitator of learning, someone who is studying to be a teacher
- Teaching – facilitation of learning
- Planning – preparation for learning

We have strived to take a common structural approach for every chapter in this book so that you, the reader, can weave in and out of different chapters and navigate your own professional development path, using identified chapters in this book to support aspects of your practice as and when they arise. In each chapter, you will find:

■ Voices of teachers and teacher educators
■ Unpicking of practice and some key terminology
■ Vignettes that shed light on classroom life (examples from practice)
■ Opportunities for reflection (points to ponder)

You will notice that we have maintained a tone that is collegiate. We regard ourselves as fellow professionals, and our chapters communicate our keenness and passion to engage with others about learning and teaching. Throughout this book, we invite you to critique accepted practice and your own understanding. We invite you to reflect, to question and to enter into dialogue with colleagues about learning and how we prepare for it through our planning. This critical engagement, we hope, serves to promote and sustain children's curiosity – both inside and outside of school. The authors in this book work with student teachers on a daily basis across a range of professional courses. Our collective experience is echoed throughout all chapters. In each chapter, we present a perspective on planning, unpick pedagogy and, most notably, translate thinking into practice through our 'examples from practice' vignettes. Our shared belief that teaching is an ongoing and evolving reflective art is evident in the 'points to ponder' that can be found at the end of each chapter. These opportunities for reflection encourage you to continue your professional development journey and can be used to help refine and hone your practice.

There are some guiding principles that underpin the chapters in this book. First, planning is influenced by our personal educational philosophy. This requires us, as teachers, to reflect upon and examine what we individually believe are the fundamental purposes and goals of schooling and education. Is it, for example, to equip the next generation with basic and vital skills necessary to sustain a workforce in the future? Or is it to instil a set of core values? Or is it to inspire our future politicians, peace-makers, environmentalists, scientists, artists, writers, athletes and technological pioneers to continue and further human development? Or perhaps to make society fairer? Our personal educational philosophy enables us to justify our pedagogical choices, and this philosophy underpins (consciously and subconsciously) every planning decision we make as teachers.

Second, the implication for many of the chapters is that planning relies on having a good professional grasp of your curriculum whilst recognising that this can develop and change. Our knowledge of curriculum (including subject knowledge) arises out of our professional reading of literature, research and legislation. This knowledge deepens through our professional discussions with colleagues and others in the educational field and can be refined through our continual engagement with recent wider societal developments. This book recognises that our grasp and interpretation of curriculum is fluid and contextual. As teachers, we need to continue to adapt and innovate our planning and practice throughout our careers to meet changing demands, children's needs and societal drivers.

The specialist knowledge of teachers is more than curriculum and subject knowledge (what we teach and what children need to learn). It includes *how* to teach (how learners learn and how we teach to support this). Some chapters in this book (in particular, Chapter 4 on lesson design) return to the first principles of planning underpinned by the belief that teachers can maintain an autonomous and professional approach when working with any published scheme or planning format. As teachers we are learners. We continually develop our knowledge of pedagogy based upon experience and reflection.

Our most important guiding principle is that planning supports the holistic development of a child, and therefore, learning opportunities should not be solely driven by legislative requirements. At the heart of the planning process is the learner; their strengths, experiences, interests and needs. Some of the chapters in this book (for example, Chapter 9 on outdoor learning) highlight the significance and place of planning for key characteristics of holistic learning such as risk-taking, resilience, critical thinking and being open to alternative ideas. Other chapters connect holistic learning with the argument for curriculum breadth and balance (for example, Chapter 12 on creativity). Chapters in this book that explore sustainability (Chapter 13) and also inclusion (Chapter 3) present a range of planning opportunities that recognise and draw from current local and global issues such as sustainable development and addressing inequalities surrounding gender, ethnicity and disability. Consequently, these chapters encourages us to plan for practices where children begin to see themselves as future citizens of a wider society, with a responsibility to contribute, protect and challenge. In planning for the holistic development of the child we recognise that one of the goals of education is to nurture active, respectful and passionate citizens of a global society.

We invite you to think about planning in its broadest sense; to consider all of the preparation for learning that teachers engage in and to review accepted practices through the lens of inclusive practice and the overall goals of education (your own and society's). We offer to you our perspectives on what constitutes purposeful planning for learning in the hope that this supports, challenges and stimulates your professional thinking about how to shape learning and teaching in the primary school.

2

Roles and responsibilities in learning

Paul Waring-Thomas and Catherine Gripton

Introduction

Before taking up a place on an Initial Teacher Education (ITE) course, most of us will have had a range of different experiences that will have shaped our thinking about what a teacher is and what they do. We are likely to have experienced some form of school education as learners ourselves and then possibly as observers or through work experience or classroom roles, seen how different teachers organise and support learning in different subjects and possibly had a go at doing some of this ourselves. All of our experiences, positive and negative, will have shaped our perceptions of how teaching works. Some of these experiences will have been inspirational, and some might have appeared to be quite pedestrian. Some experiences will have supported us in gaining confidence and trying out possibilities, and some will have resulted in us becoming inhibited and risk-averse. Some will have encouraged us to question and some to conform. In many of these instances the subject matter might have been the same, the constraints might have been the same but the outcome for the learners was different. In this chapter, we encourage you to consider, 'What sort of teacher do I want to be?' We offer some theoretical frameworks that enable us to reflect on and enhance our professional development journey. Our chapter then focuses on the role of the learner and how our planning can consciously and subconsciously reinforce different perceptions of a learner.

What sort of teacher do I want to be?

When we look at experienced teachers they often seem to be effortless in their approach. Their classrooms seem to be organised and focused, the children seem to be engaged and behaving well, the teacher seems confident and relaxed and everything just seems to happen automatically. Such a teacher might be described as 'unconsciously competent', in other words, able to complete multiple tasks at the same time, not having to think about how to respond to demands and able to pre-empt issues so that they never seem to develop into something that would derail the lesson and the learning. The beginning student teacher might look at such an experienced teacher unaware of the level of skill, knowledge and understanding underpinning such an approach within the classroom. They might think that teaching is simply a case of finding something for children to do that will occupy them, and that teaching is about how they perform rather than about how the children engage, respond and learn. Their stage of development might be termed 'unconsciously in-competent', where the beginner student teacher is unaware of the skills, knowledge and understanding that a teacher needs to be effective. In order to move from this position, the first thing that needs to happen is for the beginning student teacher to become aware of the qualities that teachers demonstrate and to recognise that these are aspects of their own practice that need to develop. Without the awareness that there are parts of a teacher's practice that can be developed and the self-awareness that these things apply to them and their own current levels of skill or competence, then such a beginner will remain 'unconsciously incompetent' and never begin the process of improvement. The model in Figure 2.1 shows a representation of the stages that learners of a skill (or set of skills, knowledge and behaviours) need to go through to the stage exhibited by experienced members of the profession.

The journey might not be easy or straightforward – it is never comfortable to recognise that there are qualities of a role that we are unable to demonstrate effectively – but with practice, reflection and guidance we can move through the stages of development identified. We can recognise our 'conscious incompetence', a state where we might be painfully aware of the fact that we cannot yet carry out the role of a teacher because there are so many aspects of practice to focus on. Once we start to become aware of these skills and open ourselves up to developing them, then we are able to increase our proficiency and move towards 'conscious competence',

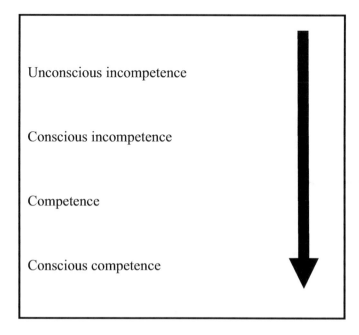

FIGURE 2.1 Conscious competency model of teacher development (adapted from Robinson 1974).

where we are able to make choices and deploy these professional attributes within the classroom to support the children that we teach. For this to happen we need to make a commitment to personal development, we need to open ourselves up to mentoring and we need to reflect upon the effectiveness of our practice. Through this it is possible to move from the conscious decision-making and deployment of skills as a teacher through to being able to do this as if it is second nature (unconscious competence).

Whether we are at an early or later stage of our teaching career, our own perceptions, values and beliefs about the teacher's role will influence the choices that we make within the classroom and, therefore, the outcomes for the children that we teach. As Hattie says, "...the ultimate requirement is for teachers to develop the skill of evaluating the effect that they have on their students" (Hattie 2012:32). In order to do this we need to look closely at the choices that we make and why we make them. Our choices are shaped by the teaching and learning experiences that we ourselves had and continue to have. They are shaped by our views about the world and our feelings (sometimes incorrect) about when teaching and learning is most effective. It can be difficult to change our beliefs about the way that we think things should be done. If we are open to experiences and new ways of working, if we are prepared to try things out and if we are able to evaluate the effect of that change, then we will have broadened the range of approaches available to us. In doing this, we will have developed our skills based upon evidence rather than assumptions. It can be uncomfortable, leading to 'cognitive dissonance' when our existing beliefs and views come into conflict with new approaches but, when resolved, will complement rather than contradict our approach to teaching and learning (Muijs & Reynolds 2018:97)

A technique through which we might do this is called the Johari window, developed by two American psychologists, Joseph Luft and Harry Ingham (the name is a synthesis of their first names), as a way of supporting people in understanding more about themselves and how they are perceived by others. Figure 2.2 offers an

	known by student teacher	unknown by student teacher
known by experienced teacher	open	blind
unknown by experienced teacher	hidden	unknown

FIGURE 2.2 A Johari's window interpretation of mentoring student teachers.

interpretation of this window for teaching. Within the Johari window there are four areas, some of which we are aware of and some which others are aware of but we are not. There are aspects of our practice and our approach that we share with others, called the open area. There are three other areas: the blind spot or blind area which others can see but we are unaware of; the hidden area containing aspects that we are aware of but others do not see this or know of it; the unknown area containing aspects not known to ourselves or to others as they see us (Luft 1961).

When working with experienced teachers who are mentoring our development, the open/free area is the one that we need to try to expand. It is the area where shared, mutually accessible discussions about existing practice take place. If we can increase the aspects of our practice that we and others are aware of we can develop our potential and open up possibilities for the future. It might be uncomfortable and a little frightening at times but if we can take risks with our teaching choices in a supportive environment, then we are likely to broaden our expertise and widen the repertoire that we can call upon as teachers rather than be limited to a narrow approach which could close down productive avenues for children, leading to a limited curriculum rather than one that is broad and balanced where all children are supported to try to achieve their potential.

Mentors can suggest development in areas of our practice that they can see but that we are unaware of. This could be aspects where we might be showing capability or aspects of practice within which we are unconsciously projecting either positive or negative behaviours. This can open up the blind areas so that we can take steps to expand our capabilities and self-monitor our approaches and responses. If we open up and share our concerns and skills with those who are supporting us then we are making the hidden area available for development and deployment. With the guidance of skilled members of the profession we can tackle areas that we might otherwise keep hidden and perhaps turn them into areas that will open up into unanticipated strengths in our practice. With a personal commitment to reflection and the support of those around us we can continue to develop into the teachers that we might want to be, realising those goals in practice and supporting the learners with whom we work.

What is the child's role in learning?

Given the number of hours most children spend in school, a surprisingly small proportion of educational research focuses upon children's experiences of school. It is an interesting question to pose as a teacher: what is it like to be an individual child in this classroom? Everyone experiences and interprets experiences differently so all children in a class will have a different lived experience of it (the meaning they each make of the experience). The implication of this is, therefore, that what we intend or plan for children to experience or learn might be quite different from what an individual child actually experiences or learns. As teachers, we need to continually observe and interact with children to assess this difference so we know what they have understood (individually) as opposed to what we have 'covered' (as a class). We can then adapt our plans in the moment as well as over time to most effectively teach the children.

Children's motivation

In planning, teachers consider children's motivation. Teachers put significant effort into providing interesting contexts, stimuli or 'hooks' which they think will engage and interest the children. This is not necessarily limited to their current interests as it can also include what they might find interesting. For example, a child who is currently 'mad about cars' can find fascination in a beautiful shell or unfamiliar poem if they are encouraged and supported to look closely, think deeply and pose questions. Children can find fascination in things that we might think are mundane and initial fascination can become a group/class interest over time where they share experiences and model interest for each other. Student teachers have reported children finding fascination in all manner of things such as the length of the drips of a leaky whiteboard pen, the hand dryer in the toilets and the rivets in the side of the school building. Planning to include stimuli and experiences which might interest children can prove highly successful for motivation and therefore learning. Example from practice 2.1 demonstrates how this can be achieved simply by looking at a familiar object in a new way and can lead to new insight for the children. The example highlights the importance of emotional engagement with learning in motivating children. It also demonstrates the crucial importance of the teacher in modelling learning behaviours and enthusiasm and how this can easily transfer to the children.

Example from practice 2.1: Reception class and the pet potato

Jane kept the children guessing for the whole morning. Something was in the shoebox on her desk, and they were excited to see what was inside. When the time came to look inside, Jane asked the children to ask yes/no questions to see if they could work it out. Eventually, she lifted the potato out of the box and there was an audible gasp from the class, "woah" said one child. Jane explained that they were going to use the potato to do an experiment. She talked about the questions she had about the potato, rubbed it on her cheek and tried to work out something else in the room that was approximately the same weight. The children helped Jane to make a maze out of the shoebox with a hole at the end to let in a little sunlight. Some children stroked the potato and cupped it gently. They all wanted 'a hold'. They asked if they could name the potato, which they did. They ceremoniously placed the potato at the darker end of the maze and put it near the window. "I wonder what will happen if we leave this for a few weeks", Jane said. In child–initiated time, a group of children asked if they could decorate the shoebox which they did with pictures and lots of letter 'p's in different colours. Some children made pictures or created story books about the adventures of the potato. At the end of the day, many parents were dragged over to see the potato; after a few weeks, the potato had sprouted and shoots were growing through the gaps in the maze walls.

There is a strong argument to suggest that we, as teachers, should be mindful of planning to use motivators such as getting a good job, achieving in statutory tests or earning lots of money in the future. This can devalue children's families (or other adults they know) and are very difficult for young children to grasp when employment is likely to be more years away than the number of years they have been alive.

There is a link here with the earlier discussion about avoiding a devaluing perception of children as deficient. It is based upon an assumption that children are getting ready to become valuable or whole rather than already being so. Regular reminders of long-term rewards such as a 'good job' or exam success can provide pressure and additional stress which inhibit learning and curtail creativity. Short-term rewards can similarly demotivate or be counter-productive to learning. An external prize is additional to the internal reward of learning and self-improvement, and can undermine it. In the example from practice 2.2, Jemma's progress in gymnastics was hampered when she knew that she was being judged. It was not that she really wanted to go to the competition (that it was a highly regarded or sought-after reward) but that she was being judged with a deadline, compared for selection, and that there was a significant chance that she might not meet the standard. She began to doubt her technique and internalised failure rather than learning from it. Essentially, she tried harder and practised more yet achieved less. Her teacher had planned to use the competition to improve learning, but this decision had backfired in Jemma's case.

Example from practice 2.2: Jemma rolls backwards

Eight-year-old Jemma was enjoying a term of gymnastics lessons in PE. Each week, she delighted in moving the coffee table out of the way and demonstrating her newly acquired skills to her family in the evening. Jemma had been able to do forward rolls for a few years but was now beginning to master the backward roll, although it was taking more effort, and not all attempts were successful. One week, Jemma's teacher announced that eight children from the class were to be selected for a gymnastics competition at the local secondary school. Jemma's teacher explained that he was looking for the children doing the best rolls in the next three lessons to select for the competition. He thought that this would motivate the children to improve the quality of their work, to practise more at home and to try their hardest in every gymnastics lesson. That evening, Jemma moved the coffee table and asked her Mum to help her do really good rolls. She quickly became agitated every time the rolls did not go quite right, and as she did more and more, fewer and fewer of them were successful. She became frustrated, "I'm never going to be able to do a backwards roll and my forwards roll is getting worser", she exclaimed. Each Tuesday evening, she went to bed saying, "It's Gymnastics tomorrow" and each Wednesday morning she was cross when her Mum said she couldn't help her practice before school as she had to go to work, "you always leave early for work", she grumbled. The evening before the final lesson, Jemma would not attempt a backwards roll, and she found that her body seemed to have forgotten how to do a forwards roll completely. She was more and more cautious each time she attempted a roll and ended up falling sideways on every one. "I am just not a Gymnastics person", she sighed. Jemma did not get selected for the competition.

Immediate rewards such as stickers and table points have been criticised for their temporary, strategic nature and ultimate ineffectiveness (Deci, Koestner & Ryan 2001), and planning to use them should be considered very carefully. When one child is publicly given a sticker then all of the other children are simultaneously not rewarded. Some children are disproportionally rewarded more than others, and consistent 'good behaviour' or attainment can be overlooked as teachers struggle to monitor equity and fairness whilst managing individual, group and class reward systems. At worst, children are led to be strategic (finding the most efficient way to get the reward) or only motivated where an incentive is offered, losing interest as soon as it has been achieved. Learning can be superficial and as short-lived as the reward. Surely it is preferable for children to be self-motivated to learn so that positive and sustainable life-long learning habits are instilled. Such intrinsic motivation maintains regardless of teacher or parental attention, and ownership of learning rests more with the child than with extrinsic rewards which are the teacher's responsibility. Teachers can plan to support children's internal motivation by modelling it for their pupils and by providing stimuli and learning experiences which challenge, engage and interest them. Considering what a child finds attractive (their currency or things they care about) is another way of thinking about rewards when planning. Making learning irresistible, including wonder and fascination in learning experiences, alongside a belief that learning is inherently beneficial (rather than merely a means to an end), leads to more sustainable learning, greater child ownership of learning and healthier learning behaviours.

Planning for the child's role in learning is ultimately shaped by our perception of children and childhood more generally. James, Jenks & Prout (1998) identified four broad conceptions of childhood. The idea that we have different conceptions of childhood suggests that these might account for differences in teachers' practice. If children are deemed a minority group in society then a teacher might give much care and assistance to children (getting resources out and giving spellings). Where teachers view children within social structures (such as gender and class) then a teacher might plan topics to appeal to boys or set homework tasks being mindful of home resources based upon perceptions of class. Where children are deemed a separate group in society (distinctly different from adults) then a teacher might see childhood as a special time, wanting to 'let the children be children', seeking to preserve play and protecting children from adult worries or concerns. If a teacher perceives children as a group constructed by society (shaped by time and cultural context) then they might recognise changes in childhood over time and seek to meet the needs of a digital generation, for example. Whilst it is too simplistic to think that any one teacher will see childhood in just one of these ways, it is helpful for us, as teachers, to reflect upon how we perceive children and how this influences our practice. If we perceive children as being competent, independent and capable then we will give them class and school responsibilities and encourage them to make choices within their learning. If we perceive children as vulnerable and with needs then we will focus upon creating feelings of safety and avoid planning pressure-laden choices that children might not be ready for yet. When planning for learning it is important to consider what messages we are communicating, sometimes subtlety and subconsciously, about the child's role in learning.

How does the child's role relate to the role of the teacher?

The relationship between the teacher and child is key in terms of the interaction between the teacher and the child's role in learning. The two interface and are shaped by the other. When planning in the shorter and longer term, teachers consider the learning experience from different children's perspectives. It can be helpful to walk an hour in a child's shoes, tracking one child as they navigate their way through schooling. Some teachers have been known to move around a classroom on their knees or spend some time sitting on the carpet or at a desk at the back (when someone else is teaching) to see what the classroom is physically like from a child's perspective. On a practical level, planning pro formas can be colour coded or split so that the teacher's and the children's experiences are considered separately. This can be enlightening where it reveals that the teacher is working harder than the children or that the children are mainly sitting and watching one child answering a question. There may be parts of the lesson which appear to be more overtly 'teacher-led' where we think that we are clear about the role of the teacher. In these parts the child's role can be very passive and they might not be actively engaged (either physically or mentally). Such exercises can also reveal that there are sections of a lesson where the teacher's role is predominantly administrative with very little 'teaching' apparently involved. Where this occurs, it can prompt us to change our plans so that the teacher is actively supporting learning and the children are actively engaged in the learning throughout the lesson. The interactive relationship between the teacher and the child's role can be acknowledged and exploited through planning in order to maximise potential for learning. The example from practice 2.3 is common to many early career and student teachers where they prepare and plan for the first part of the lesson in significant detail but are much less prepared for the middle part of the lesson. They seem less sure of their role as the teacher when they are not addressing the whole class. This suggests that more generally there are assumptions about what the teacher role is throughout the lesson. It can be useful to interrogate our perceptions of the teacher role as it assists us in planning for our role and the children's roles in learning.

Example from practice 2.3: Kat's art lesson

In conversation with Dave (her placement mentor), Kat seemed disheartened by how her art lesson went that morning which was based on a three-part lesson design. "They just didn't get it", Kat explained to Dave.

> I planned it really well and they just didn't get it. I planned questions, self-assessment and resources, just as we talked about. I spent ages on Sunday making the model picture for them. The children didn't seem to have done much oil pastel work before and some even tried to rub it out! I should have done painting instead.

Dave encouraged Kat to look over her lesson plan. It was indeed very detailed and included the stimuli, learning objective, assessment opportunities and key questions. Dave asked Kat to highlight the part of the lesson that related to her lesson introduction, and she highlighted all of the key questions and most of the lesson narrative. He then asked her which bits of her plan related to the remaining 45 minutes of the lesson. Kat paused and bashfully pointed to the line in her plan that read, 'Walk around room and check children are on task. Offer help where needed.' Kat realised that she had prepared in great depth for the first 15 minutes but had no key questions or activities planned to support, further or extend the children's learning after that point. She did not seem to know what her role was, as a teacher, when the children were working individually at the tables. The following week she planned a sketching lesson focused on use of line and planned 'pencil down' time for children to reflect and peer review through a window shopping exercise where the children toured the classroom, looking at each others' sketches before returning to their own. She planned for children to write and add to the success criteria on a flip chart, and to peer and self-assess using these success criteria throughout the lesson. Dave was thrilled to observe that Kat had planned key questions for all sections of her session and was skilfully intervening to support individual children's learning. Her plan for this lesson included possibilities and 'ifs' so that she was prepared to challenge and support individuals through questioning, modelling and feedback, and that these were explicitly linked to the learning objective. Her teacher role in the final 40 minutes of this lesson was to actively support learning rather than merely management and administration of resources as it had been the week before. The children were engaged and focused throughout the lesson, and pleased with what they had been able to achieve with several children wanting to show their artwork to their parents.

In Kat's second lesson, the role of the child is significantly more than that of a passenger along for the ride. The children were keen and motivated and were striving for improvement and, as a consequence, were working harders than the teacher. The first two sections of this chapter considered the role of the teacher and child separately, but, of course, they are entirely reliant upon each other. Children are guided as to their role in their learning through the classroom ethos, the planned activities and the role taken by the teacher (including their expectations). The teacher's beliefs and choices are crucial in shaping the child's role. Where a teacher believes that their role is to instruct then the child's role is to receive and comply. Where the teacher role is to inspire, the child's role is to respond and be creative.

Children's learning behaviours are formed by the perception of teaching enacted by the teacher. This can be thought of in terms of a 'didactic contract' (Brousseau 1997) between teacher and child in relation to the specific learning intended within a lesson or learning experience. The term originates from French mathematics education but is a useful notion for teacher reflection more generally in defining the teacher/child roles. The 'didactic contract' involves the expectations, beliefs, obligations and responsibilities of the teacher and the child within a lesson or learning experience. This has the child/teacher relationship at its heart and is therefore more than just a social relationship, it is a *learning* relationship. This includes consideration of how these responsibilities are established or agreed. As teachers we plan for the learning and the learning relationship. We must plan for both the teacher and child role within a learning experience, ensuring that these align and are also supported by appropriate structure and activities.

Points to ponder

What kind of teacher do you want to be and why?

What do you believe the teacher role to be and how has this changed over time?

To what extent do you take risks in your teaching (and what do you understand by that)?

Within a specific teaching situation, what are your responsibilities for learning and what are the children's responsibilities?

How do you perceive children and childhood and how does this impact upon your teaching choices?

References

Brousseau, G. (1997) *Theory of didactical situations in mathematics* [Edited and translated by Balacheff, N., Cooper, M., Sutherland, R. & Warfield, V.]. Dordrecht: Kluwer.

Deci, E. L., Koestner, R. & Ryan, R. M. (2001) Extrinsic rewards and intrinsic motivation in education: Reconsidered once again. *Review of Educational Research*, 71(1), 1–27.

Hattie, J. (2012) *Visible learning for teachers*. London: Routledge.

James, A., Jenks, C. & Prout, A. (1998) *Theorizing childhood*. Cambridge: Polity Press.

Luft, J. (1961) The Johari window: a graphic model of awareness in interpersonal relationships. *NTL Human Relations Training News*, 5, 6–7.

Muijs, D. & Reynolds, D. (2018) *Effective teaching: Evidence and practice*. London: Sage.

Robinson, W. L. (1974) Conscious competency – The mark of a competent instructor. *The Personnel Journal – Baltimore* 53, 538–539.

3

Inclusive planning for learning

Fiona Hunter and Natasha Serret

Introduction

This chapter explores how to plan for learning to help promote a more inclusive, informed and respectful stance towards aspects of wider societal life that serve to challenge, educate and enrich our collective mindset. In our rapidly evolving global community, where societal perceptions about gender, sexual orientation, culture, religion and disability shift constantly, a primary teacher needs to think about how they will prepare their young learners for the future. This chapter considers how to plan using inclusion as a starting point, so that young learners embrace their futures with an independent and reflective mind that is resilient and open to difference.

Creating a climate for inclusion

Inclusion is by no means a new concept within education but is one which has evolved significantly over recent years. Literature outlines how our thinking has progressed from early views about segregation (excluding groups whose needs and characteristics are perceived to be outside of the norm), to integration (including these marginalised groups but still seeing them as 'the other') through to a range of inclusive approaches. Ideally, these inclusive approaches enable society to challenge and shift views, perceptions and its infrastructure so that marginalised groups are no longer seen as 'outsiders' but, in fact, agents of significant change in societal thinking (Frederickson & Cline, 2015).

A classroom is a small community within a larger school community which, in turn, is part of a wider local community. The children we teach are part of that local, national and global community (Figure 3.1), and it is essential that we nurture a positive, valuing ethos which has the potential to impact beyond the school gates. As we seek to create an environment which promotes an inclusive philosophy we need to consider both the implicit and explicit classroom environments. All classes are comprised of unique individuals who have their own interests, preferences, challenges and barriers to learning. It is our role as the teacher to foster an

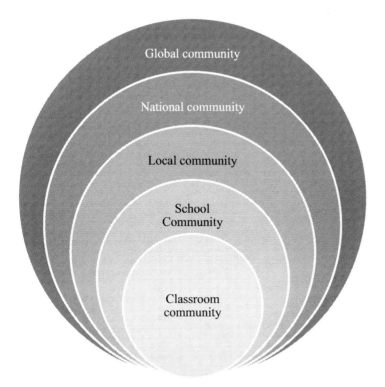

FIGURE 3.1 The classroom community.

environment whereby everyone feels a sense of belonging, has a sense of ownership and feels valued. This philosophy needs to be promoted both inside schools and outside within wider society. The approach not only encompasses those identified as vulnerable to feelings of exclusion (for example, within the protected characteristics set out in the Equality Act, 2010) but also recognises that exclusion can be felt by all. Anyone, at any point, in their lives can experience a sense of exclusion. Sometimes exclusion arises out of unintentional action – when individuals instinctively create groups in order to feel a sense of belonging and inadvertently exclude others outside of these formed groups. In other instances exclusion is intentional, targeted and deliberate – when groups make conscious decisions to act in a certain way in order to make other individuals feel isolated and excluded. In both situations, as teachers, we have significant opportunity to instil a collective set of principles and values to guide children facing these situations and to prevent them from occurring in the future. In this way, our inclusive practice has an impact both in and out of schools, for face-to-face and digital contexts.

We can introduce some core inclusive principles from the start of a school year when we establish a supportive learning environment and continue to encourage these through a range of classroom activities. Often one of the first tasks we carry out at the beginning of the school year is the construction of class rules. These often articulate the expected behaviours we, as teachers, would like to see in our classrooms. We can take the opposite approach. Children are very good at identifying the factors which influence how they work best so why not ask them what behaviours they would like to be encouraged and draw the rules from them? The example from Mark's practice illustrates this (example from practice 3.1). It is essential that we recognise that with rules come responsibilities, and these need to be acknowledged by everyone in the class. It is also important that our charter includes phrases such as 'always try to' as these acknowledge that, as human beings, we are fallible and we do not always get everything right!

Example from practice 3.1: Establishing 'Our Class Rules'

At the start of the school year Mark was keen to nurture a learning environment that would enable all the learners in his class to flourish and reach their potential. He also felt that in order to sustain the ethos and principles of such a learning environment, his would have to be a collaborative endeavour and one that was owned by the learners in the class. So, instead of introducing a set of Class Rules for the school year, Mark decided to flip this on its head and let his class take the lead. He started off by asking the class, 'What helps you to work best?' and 'What can sometimes stop you from working?' He ensured that everyone spoke in a respectful way, avoiding naming particular individuals and instead to share a more general idea like 'I sometimes don't work well when I have felt unhappy and left out at lunchtime'. He asked the class to discuss this in pairs, so that everyone felt secure and confident to share their thinking. Mark then elicited ideas from different pairs and wrote these up as a collective class poster. Mark invited all the Learning Assistants to contribute as well and offered some of his ideas so that this became a collaborative piece of work. There was a long list and Mark then asked everyone to vote for their top four, and this helped the class to appreciate the power of democracy. The votes were counted, and the result was a 'Class Charter' (Figure 3.2).

Class Charter

We learn best when our classroom is quiet	We will always try to work quietly in class
We learn best when we feel safe	We will always try to make sure our words and actions are kind
We learn best when we feel we are listened to.	We will always try to let everyone share their ideas
We learn best when we have resources to help us with our learning	We will always try to look after our resources and tidy them away when we have finished

FIGURE 3.2 Example of a class charter.

Fostering a learning environment that promotes and enables inclusion

Feeling safe, valued and part of classroom community is significant for every child. Once these core principles have been established, there are other considerations that can help innovate and refine our inclusive practice. Inclusion can be promoted and enabled through representation and class discussion as well as celebrating and welcoming difference.

Representation

All learners need to be able to recognise themselves in the examples, narratives, learning contexts and resources that they engage with in day-to-day learning. Representation is more than just making sure our teaching acknowledges religious festivals or at least one non-white, non-male significant historical figure. Representation is a continuous strive to challenge previously held notions about who was instrumental in scientific, historical and societal change and who continues to be an ambassador for 'breaking the mould'. Representation should force us to make careful choices about the range of children's literature that we have in our classrooms, and whether the main characters in these stories help to inspire or limit children's aspirations for themselves. Representation should encourage us to be mindful about the assumptions we might make about family and economic circumstances when, for example, we set a 'Mothering Sunday' card-making activity or set a piece of homework that requires computer access in the home. Representation is not a quick fix. Thoughtful planning can help children to see themselves and others outside of their community beyond the confines and stereotypical images sometimes perpetuated by wider society, media and news headlines.

Celebrating and welcoming difference

There are opportunities to promote difference when planning our classroom environment. We might ensure that a range of languages are used in classroom displays and labels, for example, or designate registration as a time when children are encouraged to use different languages. In this way we are planning opportunities that help all children to appreciate language diversity and see this as a strength and not a limiting factor. Chapter 7 provides support with how to plan to support children for whom English is an Additional Language.

One way to celebrate difference is to encourage each child to complete a culture wheel. Each child completes a blank circle divided into five sections by drawing or writing one thing in each section about their family life in relation to food/interests/celebrations/values/music (what is important for me and my family). Culture wheels can initiate classroom conversations about the cultural characteristics of different children and help the children to see that everyone is culturally different. It can also help children to recognise that, regardless of our differences, some aspects (for example, supporting a football team) can unite us. Culture wheels, especially if done at the start of an academic year, should help to inform our planning. Knowing the interests and expertise of our individual learners provides some relevant contexts and starting points for our planning across the curriculum.

Planning for classroom discussion

Inclusion offers an opportunity to plan for classroom discussions that tap into wider societal issues. Children will encounter current challenges that society might be experiencing that relate to culture, religion, gender, sexual orientation and disability through a number of sources. These include the media, the internet, the local community and in the day-to-day conversations with immediate and wider family. A range of perspectives, some conflicting, will be represented through these experiences. How children view difference in wider society is influenced by these sources from outside school. Engaging with classroom discussions about difference in wider society can be an important, challenging, sensitive and rewarding learning and teaching experience.

When planning for classroom discussions where a societal (possibly controversial) issue is the context, consider first the purpose of this discussion. We can plan for these opportunities carefully, paying attention to relevant curriculum contexts and introducing our discussions as part of a lesson. A learning opportunity might create the possibility to establish, articulate and reinforce some of the values that lie at the heart of many different groups in society. These are enshrined in core principles that underpin different faiths (for example, The Five Pillars in Islam and The Ten Commandments in Judaism and Christianity), and therefore, the discussion might take place during Religious Education. Values also underpin different national legislative documents (for example, The Constitution of the United States or British Values) and fundamental legal frameworks (The Equality Act, The Human Rights Act, UN Convention on the Rights of the Child). Discussions could be planned for as part of a History or Personal, Social, Health and Economic education lesson. The purpose of these kinds of classroom discussions might be to help children to develop an appreciation that different people within any society can hold different perspectives on particular issues. Through the introduction of ideas such as conflict between values held by different cultures and the impact that this can have on cohesion within local and wider communities or the debates surrounding the rights and legislative consequences of the trans-gender community, we have an opportunity to instil an awareness that we can have different and often contradictory views. Careful planning will encourage children to become open to and engage with these different views and nurture the acceptance that their view might be different to that of others. These discussions enable children to see themselves as future citizens of a wider, bigger society and ideally empower them to realise that they will have an important role in continuing to shape and influence society. In summary, the purpose of classroom discussions, where current issues relating to inclusion form the context, is to develop:

- An appreciation of different perspectives
- An awareness that personal views can contradict with each other
- An acceptance that their view might be different to the views of others, including their peers
- A realisation of their role as future citizens in a bigger society

Our example from Maria's practice illustrates how this might work in the classroom (example from practice 3.2).

Example from practice 3.2: Maria reads *And Tango makes three*

Maria sat with her class of 6–7 years olds and shared the book *And Tango makes three* (Richardson & Parnell, 2007). She started off by showing the picture on the front cover of two penguins and a baby penguin and asked, 'What do you think the story is about?' She then read the story, slowly, carefully and sensitively. She observed different children as she shared this picture book, based on a true story about two male penguins who lived in Central Park Zoo, New York, and who were in love. They were given an opportunity to raise a baby penguin from an egg abandoned by its mother. After reading the story, the teacher looked up. She asked the class to turn and face their talk partners, and asked the class three questions:

- Which part of the story did you enjoy and why?
- What do you think the story is about?
- Was there anything about the story that surprised you?

These questions (coupled with having the opportunity to discuss these in pairs first) helped to establish a comfortable, non-threatening learning environment that could support a sensitive discussion. The questions also opened up the space for a discussion about different views on same-sex relationships and how core values such as respect and tolerance can help guide our responses to this.

Identifying the key learning opportunities

As a consequence, the opportunity to promote an inclusive ethos can occur within all of our teaching and daily classroom interactions. Whilst some of these might arise spontaneously (for example, an incident at playtime) and require us to respond in the moment, we still need to take time to think and plan how to use all opportunities effectively. We need to think about and plan for what will be the specific focus of any experience. The planning might anticipate the possibility to develop and promote particular values such as tolerance and respect. There might be a chance to plan some individual reflective writing that captures personal perspectives on sensitive issues. The learning might help to address a particular social or emotional issue that has arisen in class. Or the context might provide an opportunity to highlight key social and/or historical milestones that shaped our inclusive society today (for example, women's rights or the civil rights movement). The important implication here is that the focus is anticipated, planned for and handled with sensitivity and care.

Points to ponder

Review a classroom or educational setting, considering representation within the learning environment. How representative are the books, resources, games and images? Are stereotypes challenged through representation? What is the balance of representation of different families, gender roles, languages, religions and disability?

Create a mind map of some of the key historical milestones and figures that you feel have shaped our society to help create a more inclusive ethos. How could you introduce and celebrate some of these within your classroom? What would your specific learning intention be?

Identify a children's book or an extract from children's literature that you feel helps to communicate a core inclusive principle. Think about how you could use this as a resource to stimulate a classroom discussion around inclusion. What key questions would you ask? What kinds of follow-up activities would you implement to develop understanding?

As a powerful role model for the children you teach, how do you model inclusivity for the children?

Reflecting on the verbal and non-verbal interactions you have with children, to what extent does the language you use, the tone of your voice and your non-verbal communication, value them and all people in society?

References

Equality Act (2010) [online]. Available at www.legislation.gov.uk/ukpga/2010/15/contents

Frederickson, N. & Cline, T. (2015) *Special educational needs, inclusion and diversity*. Maidenhead: Open University Press.

Richardson, J. & Parnell, P. (2007) *And Tango makes three*. New York: Simon and Schuster.

4

Principles of lesson design

Simon Brown, Laura Malpas and Nick Mills

Introduction

In this chapter, we focus on essential aspects of lesson design which are common to many planning formats. We explore what it is that makes an effective lesson design, through seven principles. These are certainly not the only principles that might be discussed, but they are some of the important ones. Other key aspects such as planning for additional needs and planning for assessment are explored thoroughly in dedicated chapters elsewhere in this book. Although sometimes perceived as time-consuming and repetitive, lesson planning is a process whereby teachers identify the 'essentials' of a lesson, so that it becomes part of a natural process and influences thinking. In this chapter, we recognise designing a lesson as a professional craft, so that our pedagogical choices are rooted in learning.

Preparing detailed lesson plans supports our professional development and acts as a 'comfort-blanket', especially during observed lessons. All aspects of any lesson plan format should scaffold the thinking process which the teacher has followed in considering the lesson. By going through this process you are reminding yourself and reassuring any observer about the breadth of thinking when considering the needs of the curriculum and the class. Over time, there have been a number of recommended lesson structures, suggested by different initiatives. All have some merit in changing practice, but it is most important to understand the principles which underpin successful lesson design. Understanding these principles will support you in interpreting and working with any lesson design, allowing you to use the design to plan and teach as an autonomous professional.

Throughout our discussion of our seven principles we draw upon examples from a few lessons. In particular, we make reference to a mathematics lesson, for children aged 7–10 years. This lesson is based upon a 'Magic Vs' investigation (Nrich 2019). In the investigation, children are asked to place the numbers 1 to 5 in a 'V' formation so that both arms have the same total. You may wish to explore this activity, through the link given at the end of this chapter, before reading on.

This could be seen as an example of a 'low threshold; high ceiling' activity (Nrich 2011), in that the majority of children at this age could cope with the calculation skills needed (the threshold is low), but higher attaining children could still be challenged to work systematically, make conjectures and explain their thinking to a high level (the ceiling is high!).

Principle 1: Have clarity about objectives

The first questions to answer when planning a lesson are, 'What do I want the children to learn?' or 'What skill do I want them to develop?' If we start here, the planning process will be led by learning, rather than by an activity that happens to have taken our fancy.

According to Echevarría, Vogt and Short (2008), one of the characteristics of effective instruction is that it is guided by 'concrete [...] objectives that identify what students should know and be able to do' (p. 24). Most lesson plan formats have a section entitled 'Learning Objective'. This could also be called learning intentions or learning aims. Here, the main aim of the lesson should be made clear. It is important to note that learning objectives have their origin in the curriculum being followed by the school, and so are part of a greater plan for learning over time. The learning objective should build on what the children have learned previously. David Ausubel (in Novak & Gowin 1984) tells us that 'what students already know is the most important factor in what they can learn'. Allowing pupils to make connections to prior learning supports their understanding. It is also important to make sure that we create learning objectives which are context-free, specific and transferable; they are not descriptions of a task but of learning.

Then there is the question of how the teacher and the children will know that the learning objective has been achieved, in other words, the 'success criteria'. The following example 4.1 illustrates the relationship between learning objective and success criteria in a lesson plan for the 'Magic Vs' investigation:

Example from practice 4.1: The relationship between the learning objective and success criteria

Success Criteria:

Have a way of finding all the possibilities (may be trial and improvement)

State a simple rule (What do you notice?)

Convince a friend that the rule will always work

Some children may ask a 'What if …?' question, make a further conjecture and test it out.

Learning objective: to discover and explain a rule.

In the example above, the success criteria would focus on aspects of mathematical thinking which the children need to develop, rather than other skills such as accurate addition of single digit numbers, which will be used in the lesson but which most of the children may already be expected to be quite fluent with. Equally, the success criteria should not be confused with a list of everything the children need to do, but should be key points that they need to remember, or that adults working with them should prompt them towards. Nor should they be so prescriptive as to take thinking and decision-making away from the children. Again, a knowledge of prior learning will help us to identify what these key points will be. For example, a class of children aged 9–10 years writing persuasively may already be familiar with the idea of using convincing facts and persuasive vocabulary, but less familiar with devices such as rhetorical questions, in which case the success criteria would focus on the latter.

Children's input can enhance the use of success criteria in lessons, in that when checking for understanding, additional criteria can be added or wording changed. Reference can be made to these criteria during the lesson to support the learning (mini-plenaries). These can sometimes be considered as 'steps to success' and contribute to independent learning. It is important that each of these criteria is measurable, so the child and the teacher can assess, preferably during the lesson, whether the objective was met or not.

Having considered learning objectives and success criteria, we should have a clear answer to our first question, 'What learning gains do we want to achieve?' The next question is about how to achieve them.

Principle 2: Ensure structural alignment

What we are calling the principle of structural alignment, a term inspired by the idea of 'constructive alignment' (Biggs & Tang, 2007), should not be applied so as to stifle children's creativity. For example, open questions, open tasks and the opportunity for children to make decisions play an important part in effective lesson design. Nevertheless, in an effectively structured lesson:

- The learning objectives
- Success criteria
- Teacher explanations and modelling
- Tasks that children carry out
- The feedback given to children

should all be aligned. The structure of the lesson, whatever form it takes, should support a logical flow of ideas and thinking, which helps the children to achieve the desired outcomes.

An example of the structure of the 'Magic Vs' lesson is included here as an example from practice 4.2:

Example from practice 4.2: Structure of a 'Magic Vs' lesson

Introduction	The teacher displays two Vs, one magic and not, and poses the questions, 'What's the same? What's different?' Suggestions are discussed. If necessary, the teacher prompts by suggesting children look at the total for the Vs and the total for the arms.
	The task is introduced and explained (find all the possible Magic Vs). Children are asked to tell their partner what they are trying to find out and discuss how they might go about it.
Paired investigation	Children explore solutions with a partner, using digit cards. The teacher questions and prompts as appropriate. After an appropriate amount of time there is discussion about what constitutes a 'different' Magic V. (For example, if the arms are simply swapped, this may be classed as the same V.) The teacher looks for children who:

- Are struggling for a strategy
- May not understand odd and even numbers
- Are not using the associative rule
- Have found the solutions and are beginning to come up with a rule

Mini-plenary	Ideas and strategies are shared, and learning assessed, based on the observations from above. The teacher may model their own thinking or choose a child to model theirs.
Paired investigation	Continued investigation and recording of findings. Some children may be able to explain what they have discovered and move onto a planned extension question. Some may need support, for example, reinforcement of odd and even numbers. Resources are available to support intervention if necessary.
Plenary and reflection	Discuss and explain findings. Encourage children to rephrase and explain in their own words what they have discovered.
	What reasoning skills did they use? How could they improve their work? What have they learnt for next time?

The following scenario 4.3, drawn partly from experience of working with student teachers, may help to illustrate further the idea of structural alignment. We would encourage you to read through the outline and reflect on the questions before reading on.

Example from practice 4.3: Lesson demonstrating structural alignment

Learning objective: Subtract 2-digit numbers from 2-digit numbers

Introduction	The teacher begins the lesson with a short starter, during which children are asked to find pairs of numbers which add to make 10.
Whole class teaching: task 1	The teacher models how a 100 square can be used to find the difference between two 2-digit numbers. He makes use of the structure of the 100 square, showing how the columns increase in tens whilst the rows increase in ones. For example, to find the answer to 47 − 25 he models how to 'count up' in tens from 25, and then in ones from 45, to find the difference ("10, 20, 21, 22").

21	22	23	24	25	26	27	28	29	30
31	32	33	34	35	36	37	38	39	40
41	42	43	44	45	46	47	48	49	50

Independent work   The children are then asked to solve a series of similar subtraction calculations. They are provided with number lines in order to support them in finding the difference between the pairs of 2-digit numbers by counting up from the smallest number to the largest number.

Plenary   In a plenary, the teacher goes through the answers and asks the children to mark their own work. Some time is given for children to correct any mistakes, whilst those who have fully grasped the lesson objective are given a word problem to solve: "There are 52 children on a coach. At the first stop, 11 children get off. How many children are now on the coach?"

After the lesson   The teacher reviews the work and makes written comments on some books, such as "Neat work" and "You got a lot done today – well done!"

Questions for reflection

■ How well does this lesson create alignment between the learning objective, the whole class teaching and the independent work?

■ How helpful is the plenary in building on what has gone before?

■ How might the feedback be better aligned to the learning objective?

Having considered these questions, you may have reflected on the following points:

■ The starter, by refreshing the children's memories about number bonds to ten, may have supported them when counting up on the number line and 'bridging' through multiples of ten.

■ There might have been closer alignment between the whole class teaching (using a 100 square) and the independent work (when the children were supported by number lines). It may have been more effective for the teacher to model using the same resource which children were going to be using later in the lesson. (Alternatively, if the children were already familiar with using a number line, an explicit connection and comparison might have been made between the two resources.)

■ The plenary was helpful in that it gave the children opportunity to apply their subtraction skills to a real-life situation. However, it could be argued that the word problem might have been more closely aligned if it had used a situation which encouraged the children to think more in terms of 'difference', rather than 'take-away', as difference was the model of subtraction being focused on in this lesson. For example, "31 children in Year 2 have school dinners; 25 have packed lunches. How many more children have school dinners?" (Of course, the teacher may have been deliberately choosing to move children's thinking on to consider an alternative model, in preparation for the next lesson.)

■ The feedback would have been more closely aligned if specific comments had been given, related to the learning objective, and moving children who have achieved the objective on to a next step.

Principle 3: Use key ideas to structure a lesson

Many of us have probably taught a lesson and reflected that the pace was too slow, or that children spent too long listening to the teacher at the beginning of the session. Sometimes, this may be because insufficient thought has been given, at the planning stage, about what exactly the children need to learn, meaning that too long is spent on talk or activities which do not directly support the learning objective. We need to identify what the children need to learn in this lesson – the key ideas – and focus on these. Moreover, we might identify that children need to learn certain things at the beginning of a lesson, before attempting some independent or group work, and then learn more from the teacher as the lesson progresses.

Dividing a lesson into sections or 'chunking' a lesson to allow for questioning and discussion at different points during the learning can be helpful, allowing children to take small steps towards a larger learning objective. Again, it is important to consider the alignment of the different 'chunks', making sure each step builds logically upon the next, and considering the flow of thought which children need to move through to achieve the desired outcome.

For example, imagine an English lesson in which the learning objective is to write descriptive sentences including similes. The teacher's preparation may include asking themselves, 'What are my thought processes when I'm trying to achieve this?' They may decide that one way of approaching it is to think the following:

- What feature of a setting do I want to describe? (e.g. a snowy field)
- What adjectives describe that feature? What senses can I use to think of a range of ideas? (e.g. white, smooth, pure, sparkling, soft, freezing, crisp, soft)
- What else can be described by using any of those adjectives? (e.g. wool, icing, diamonds)
- How could I use some of those ideas to write a sentence about the feature which includes a simile? (e.g. The field was covered with snow, like pure white icing.)

The 'chunks' of the lesson might then be aligned to guide children through this thought process, for example, by working in small groups to:

- Mind map a range of adjectives to describe some given features
- Add to the mind map other things that could be described using those same adjectives
- Choose ideas from this mind map to create an effective descriptive sentence which includes a simile

This way, the chunks will be aligned in the sense of logical progression towards achieving the learning objective, and a possible way of approaching individual attempts to write such sentences will have been modelled.

Principle 4: Consider the role of the child

One of the key drivers in lesson design should be a focus on what children are thinking. We plan for learning, not activities. Our focus is on the children, not

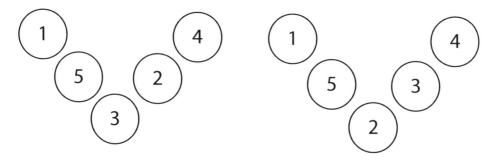

FIGURE 4.1 Example and non-example (correct and incorrect) for magic Vs lesson.

the teacher. Effective lessons scaffold children's thinking to move them from their prior learning to the desired learning outcome. It is not the material itself which is important but how the children construct their understanding. Hattie (2012:18) suggests that "teachers need to be aware of what each and every student in their class is thinking and what they know". This sounds like a daunting, yet admirable, goal and suggests that *listening* is a key driver in designing a successful lesson. As teachers, when designing a lesson, we ask ourselves, "What will it look like if a child understands?" which enables us to ask appropriate questions, listen for clues and probe thinking. We ask ourselves, "How can I support them in this process?" This could be through careful questioning or scaffolding, grouping or pupil talk as well as through the careful selection of resources, examples and tasks. This principle emphasises the importance that we plan for the time and opportunity for children to make connections through articulating and reviewing their own thinking.

At the start of a lesson, it is useful to remind children about prior learning so that important links are made. Hattie (2012:25) claims that expert teachers "combine the introduction of new subject knowledge with students' prior knowledge". This part of the lesson could include an exploration of key vocabulary or a familiar problem presented in a new context. In maths lessons, one approach is the use of questions such as "What do you notice? What do you wonder? Which is the Odd One Out? What is the same? What is different?" These questions are designed to draw attention to the key structures whilst also being non-threatening and open-ended, giving children a chance to formulate and articulate their own thinking. Used at the start of a lesson, they can encourage children to notice details, make connections and ask their own questions.

For example, in the 'Magic Vs' lesson mentioned earlier the questions, 'What's the same? What's different?' can be used to generate discussion around a correct and incorrect completed example (Figure 4.1).

Example: both arms add up to the same total of 9; non-example: both arms do not add up to the same total.

Principle 5: Choice of examples is important

An important consideration is the careful choice of examples that are used to illustrate and support a learning objective. An effective lesson design will consider how to provide a range of examples which highlight the key feature of a concept as well as a range of non-examples. So, if children are presented with a range of squares of different sizes, colours and orientations and a range of shapes which share some, but not all, of the key features (e.g. right angles, equal sides) but are also varied in size, colour and orientation they could focus on the key ingredients of a square. This approach encourages children to see what makes a square a square and eliminate the common misconception that a square turned on its end is a diamond! Here, we might again consider the importance of subject knowledge research. This leads to an understanding of potential misconceptions, as "...teachers with knowledge of the common misconceptions can plan lessons to address potential misconceptions before they arise, for example, by comparing examples to non-examples when teaching new concepts" (From Education Endowment Foundation: Improving Mathematics in Key Stages Two and Three, 2017).

Principle 6: Choice of resources is also important

As teacher subject knowledge is a key element which feeds into effective lesson design, it is useful if we have spent a little time working on the problem or concept and considered different ways in which children might approach the work. We can then identify resources to provide support, possibly for specific previously identified needs or in case a need should arise during a lesson. It is important that the resources we choose support the learning outcome and are not used for their own sake; the use of concrete resources will not in itself guarantee learning. In the 'Magic Vs' lesson, the teacher chose to use digit cards so that children could experiment freely with solutions and not become disheartened by recording lots of 'failed' attempts.

One way of developing the 'Magic Vs' lesson, after investigating all the possibilities, is to pose the question, 'What do you notice about all the Magic Vs?', leading to

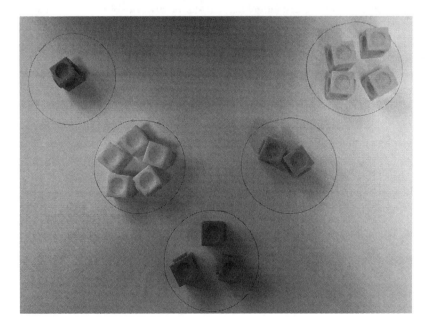

FIGURE 4.2 Cubes in a magic V.

a recognition that they all have an odd number at the bottom, and reasoning about why this is. It could be difficult for children to find this rule if they do not have a depth of understanding about odd and even numbers. With well-researched subject knowledge, we can anticipate and plan for this challenge, selecting the resource that most effectively supports children to generalise. In this case cubes (Figure 4.2) could provide a way of visually representing why an odd number needs to be at the bottom of the V, and a way of explaining rules about adding odd and even numbers. Asking children to use manipulatives and visual images to prove or explain a concept is a powerful tool in developing understanding.

Principle 7: Plan for classroom dialogue and precise use of vocabulary

Discussion and pupil talk are important elements to incorporate into a lesson, allowing children to clarify their own thinking with reference to others. Identifying key questions at the planning stage enables the teacher to probe and guide children's thinking and to assess learning during the lesson. One of our key roles, as teachers, is to model and scaffold the dialogue, and thinking, listening and giving feedback to support and extend understanding. Modelling thinking is a powerful tool and can demonstrate to children how to question themselves and develop as independent learners. Children can be encouraged to ask themselves questions such as, "How am I going to do this? What else could I try? What is working well? What similar problems have I solved?" Questions such as these can be displayed, referred to and used as prompts. Another powerful technique is to encourage pupils to clarify their ideas by repeating or rephrasing someone else's explanation in order to reinforce the correct vocabulary and develop their own understanding.

Encouraging children to express key concepts and use precise and correct vocabulary is also important. If children have the correct vocabulary, it is much easier for them to explain their thinking and demonstrate their understanding. It is particularly important when everyday vocabulary can create ambiguity. For example, when a child says, "that sound goes down," we cannot be sure whether the child is talking about pitch or volume, without further probing of the vocabulary. Supporting children to arrive at their own definitions helps to develop deeper understanding than if we provide them with ready-made definitions. More on planning questions can be found in Chapter 6.

Conclusion

The seven principles discussed in this chapter may be more useful for planning for effective teaching and learning than any one prescribed lesson structure. They can be applied to the different structures that teachers may choose between, or that may be imposed by a particular scheme of work. Your school may base their work on a published text book, but thoughtful teachers will still consider these seven principles, and make the text book work for them, rather than being constrained by what a published scheme dictates.

Points to ponder

How will I consider these principles of lesson design when engaging with a scheme of work?

How can I use the seven principles of lesson design to help make informed, professional and autonomous decisions when working with a published text book?

References

Biggs, J. & Tang, C. (2007) *Teaching for quality learning at university.* New York: McGraw-Hill Education.

Echevarria, J., Vogt, M. & Short, D. (2008) Making content comprehensible for English learners: The SIOP model. London: Pearson.

Education Endowment Foundation (2017) *Improving mathematics in key stages two and three: Guidance Report.* London: Education Endowment Foundation.

Hattie, J. (2012) *Visible learning for teachers.* London: Routledge.

Nrich, (2011) *Using low threshold, high ceiling tasks.* Available at: https://nrich.maths.org/7701

Novak, J. D. & Gowin, D. B. (1984) *Learning how to learn.* Cambridge: Cambridge University Press.

Acknowledgement

Nrich (2019). *Magic V's.* Reproduced with kind permission of NRICH, University of Cambridge. Available at: https://nrich.maths.org/6274

5

Assessment and planning for progress

Natasha Serret, Liz Ruston and Rob Perkins

Introduction

In this chapter, we take the stance that assessment should drive, inform and shape our long-, medium- and short-term planning. This places learning (the understanding, knowledge, skills and attitudes that we want learners to gain) at the heart of planning where assessment of this learning drives our pedagogical decisions and interactions. This chapter explores some of the key definitions that underpin our professional understanding of assessment. It then translates these theoretical principles of assessment into planning and practice, providing a framework that promotes an approach to planning where assessment is integral to the design of a lesson and a sequence of lessons. Our chapter helps to address some common questions about assessment for teachers:

- How do I determine the right learning objective (what I want the children to gain)? How do I know this is sufficiently challenging but still achievable?
- What kinds of learning experiences could create rich opportunities that will allow the children in my class to demonstrate what they know and can do, prior to and during a lesson?
- How will I know if the children have made progress?
- What kinds of evidence can I collect to enable me to capture and assess this learning? How will I use this evidence to judge and evidence progress?
- How much flexibility is there in my planning (and my teaching) for me to respond and act on unplanned for learning?

Within this discussion, we highlight the relevance of initial assessment **and** the power of 'in the moment' classroom evidence and feedback that supports progress in learning. Effective assessment practice relies on an interplay of evidence of prior understanding and day-to-day 'in the moment' classroom evidence that arises during lessons. Most crucially, it is how we act on this combined assessment information that makes our planning purposeful and effective in terms of children's learning.

Definitions

There are some key definitions surrounding assessment, and having a good grasp of these can inform and influence our planning. Following the seminal work of Black and Wiliam (1998), some clear distinctions were identified that clarify the purpose and audience of different kinds of assessment. Understanding these (how they differ and how they relate to each other) can also help us to be clear about our role and, more crucially, the role of the learner for these different assessment processes.

Formative Assessment (FA) is defined as any assessment practice where the evidence of learning informs teaching, planning and learning, both 'in the moment' (during a lesson) and after (planning for the next lesson). Formative assessment is thus an over-arching description of a range of teaching and learning opportunities (for example, questioning, classroom talk, group tasks/presentation/posters, self- and peer-assessment tasks) that reveal a learner's current understanding and act as a mechanism to help learning develop further. The Black Box Assessment for Learning series (e.g. Harrison & Howard 2009) has helped to establish the concept of formative assessment. This is now embedded within what is considered effective practice in schools. Our understanding of formative assessment has evolved through the ongoing research, writing and thinking of many in the educational community. This includes what are the most effective learning interactions that enable formative assessment (see Serret, Correia & Harrison 2018) and the challenges arising from this (see Earle 2017).

Many schools now refer to formative assessment as **Assessment for Learning (AfL)**. AfL encompasses a range of classroom resources and approaches (e.g. traffic lights, peer-assessment, two stars and a wish) that, when used meaningfully (to inform and enrich learning), helps us as teachers to make professional judgements about what learners 'know, half know and don't know' (Harrison 2015 in Serret, Correia & Harrison 2018). These approaches rely on classroom evidence (written, pictorial, oral). This evidence represents learning, and an interpretation of this evidence (often informed by existing curricula expectations and criteria) supports the learner and the teacher (the audience) in identifying next steps in learning. Later on in this chapter we unpick some of these approaches and consider the extent to which specific strategies, when planned for, meet this desired purpose and serve the needs of the intended audience. When planned with this purpose in mind, AfL is the answer to some of our earlier questions, 'How will I know if my learners have made progress?' and 'What kinds of evidence can I collect to enable me to capture and assess this learning? How will I use this evidence to judge and evidence progress?'

A key characteristic of formative assessment is its **validity.** The activities, contexts and approaches used to generate evidence of learning for formative assessment purposes tend to occur in authentic classroom settings, as part of a lesson and designed so that the learner is integral to the process. Consequently, the evidence is considered to be valid; a true reflection of what a learner can achieve.

Summative Assessment (SA) is defined as any assessment practice that sums up learning. This summary judgement can take many forms: a summative account of achievement in writing in a controlled setting (e.g. an extended piece of writing a test score, a reading level, a degree classification or a determination of attainment against a goal or levelled criteria). Summative assessment will occur at specified points across the academic journey for a learner (end of school phase, year, semester or term). The audience for this covers many stakeholders in education, and these include the learner, the teacher, senior management, parents and governors. The results can sometimes be published nationally or internationally and thus shared with a wider audience (usually anonymised).

A key characteristic of summative assessment is its **reliability**. For instance, summative assessment tasks have to be carefully designed so that there is minimal opportunity for different interpretations of particular questions or tasks. This ensures that these tasks can tap into specific subject knowledge and understanding. Particular attention is paid to noting the extent to which the learner completed these tasks unaided or needed teacher/peer support. Many national tests are standardised and marked externally so that teacher bias or subjectivity is removed. Tests are generalised and can be repeated multiple times across countries. Many external stakeholders (including parents, the public and future employers) value these summative achievements, and they can help to inform key decisions like university admissions, job applications and transitions into new stages of learning.

Summative AND formative assessment

Many researchers (see Dolin et al. 2018) working in the field of assessment acknowledge the role and value of both formative and summative assessment. They suggest that formative and summative assessment do not need to be regarded as mutually exclusive practices and certainly should not be seen to compete for classroom time and focus. Many teachers, however, do still feel this pressure, and this manifests itself in the conversations surrounding how teachers feel that they are simply 'teaching to the test' or 'getting children to jump through assessment hoops'. As a teacher, it is important that we understand the intentions, procedures and strategies of both forms of assessment. One way of seeing the two within the bigger picture of professional understanding is through a framework where a teacher's grasp of the subject discipline, planning, pedagogy and assessment are seen as interconnected (Black & Wiliam 2018). All elements are equally important, and each relies on the other. The relationship between planning and assessment, explored in this chapter, is key.

Where does assessment fit into the planning process?

This question is fundamental to ensuring that, as teachers, we effectively embed assessment into our daily practice. A common misconception is that assessment is the end point, something that we do after learning has taken place, something that will then be useful to judge the progress that has been made or help us to inform our next sequence of lessons. Whilst this view is, to an extent, true it also potentially limits learning. Effective practice relies upon accurate assessment as a starting point for planning. So assessment needs to be viewed much more as the first step in the planning process, not just something that is a useful by-product of learning. This enables us to focus on ensuring that we begin with an assessment of children's current understanding (starting points) and how they understand. As teachers, we learn from this and plan from this informed perspective.

What does initial assessment look like?

The range of strategies available to us as primary practitioners to gather initial assessment information is almost endless. These activities are deployed at the start of a topic, new focus or lesson, and are designed to elicit (find out) what children already know before teaching commences. For example, in primary science, activities such as 'Concept Cartoons' (Naylor & Keogh 2000) are set where children work in talk partners or small groups and discuss the concepts (and misconceptions) represented by the different characters in the cartoon about the focus area in science (e.g. thermal insulation). Karl's example from practice 5.1 illustrates this.

Example from practice 5.1: Karl and the concept cartoon

Karl decided to use concept cartoons to elicit what his class might already know about thermal insulation before the start of his science topic on 'keeping things warm'. Karl established a learning environment at the start of the lesson where he emphasised that there is 'no right or wrong answer' and that the focus was on being able to 'explain your thinking'. He gave out the concept cartoon to the class so that the children could talk about their thinking in groups of three. He also reminded the class about the importance of listening to and valuing everyone's ideas in their discussion groups. This created a learning climate where talking and sharing ideas was encouraged and celebrated.

In the cartoon, there was an image of a snowman wearing a coat and then images of several children, each with a different idea about whether the coat will or will not stop the snowman from melting. During the discussion, the children talked in their threes about which children in the cartoon they agreed and disagreed with. They expressed their own thoughts such as 'keeping the coat on the snowman will stop him from melting' and giving their reasons for thinking this. Karl moved around the groups, listening, making a note of the ideas shared and encouraging learners to keep sharing their thinking. This gave Karl a clear picture of the children's prior understanding and experiences of thermal insulation. After 15 minutes of discussion, Karl began a whole class discussion so that he could draw together the range of thinking from the class. The endpoint of this whole class discussion was not one where Karl then shared 'the right answer'. Instead, this discussion was used as a starting point for an investigation where, in the next science lesson, the class worked as 'scientists' to investigate which materials are good thermal insulators or conductors for their snowman ice-cubes. Karl felt much more prepared for the next lesson, knowing the range of existing thinking of the children in his class.

As teachers, we should not base our initial assessments of children's starting points on too narrow a footing. In other words, we must ensure we have a strong rationale for our assessments based on more than one simple piece of evidence. A case in point here would be a teacher who decided that a whole group of children were at a certain point in their understanding of fractions based solely on a review of one child's work from the previous term. In order to ensure a validity to our assessment we must ensure we have a rich and varied evidence base. The best practitioners will draw upon a number of sources of assessment evidence in order to make informed decisions that then impact on their planning. A none-exhaustive list of initial assessment sources might include some listed in Table 5.1.

TABLE 5.1 The possibilities and pitfalls of some important assessment sources

Assessment source	Brief description	Possibilities: *What evidence of learning can I expect?*	Pitfalls: *How will I know?*
Use of 'cold tasks'	Any task (see example from practice 5.1) set before formal teaching of a topic/lesson	A valid account of what children think and know before engaging with a lesson/topic	Some children benefit from a pre-teach/short introduction/ opportunity for paired talk about the learning to help them make the links with their prior experiences and learning. If the task is set too 'cold' then these children might not share a complete account of what they already know.
Work scrutiny	A structured and professional observation of a selected (or class) sample of work for a given area.	A close scrutiny of work allows teachers the chance to focus on specific evidence and match this against assessment/success criteria. Looking across a sample of children's work can give a good sense of progression in learning.	Without any knowledge of the child and the context of the learning that framed the work being scrutinised can be problematic and make it difficult to make a full and valid judgement of what this evidence of learning tells us.
Elicitation activities	An activity designed, usually as part of a lesson, to find out what children already know about a subject/topic area before teaching this area. Elicitation activities can be prompted by a stimulus such as a concept cartoon, artefact, children's book or relevant image/photograph.	The evidence can be visual (whole class mapping of ideas), individual (written reflection after the task) or oral (discussions arising from the task). If the elicitation activity is presented in a non-threatening, creative and stimulating form then the evidence can be a highly valid account of what learners know.	A key pitfall is that sometimes these activities and the evidence generated are captured in the lesson without then going on to inform the subsequent planning and teaching for the subject/topic.
Discussion with colleagues	A professional dialogue with colleagues relating to individual children, groups or the whole class.	Professional dialogue with learning support assistants, other teachers who have taught the children previously and other specialists/ colleagues who work with the children can provide an insight not captured in other assessment tasks	Dialogue can be subjective, based on other professionals' experiences with different children. It is important to listen and act on this information objectively.

(Continued)

Assessment source	Brief description	Possibilities: *What evidence of learning can I expect?*	Pitfalls: *How will I know?*
Classroom observation	Any opportunity, where the teacher distances themselves from direct teaching (however brief) and, instead, observes the learning. This could be group work or an individual context. Notes are brief and non-threatening (sticky notes can be useful). Observations need to note the lesson context, what was observed (not any assumptions of learning made from these) and thoughts/responses/next steps. This is a regular and strong feature in pedagogical documentation with younger children.	These observations take place 'in the moment' of learning and teaching. The evidence is authentic, dynamic and responsive to the teaching taking place. They can celebrate big and small significant moments in learning.	The challenge for any teaching is using our professional expertise to recognise significant moments in learning in action. What is noticed during a lesson and then recorded can be highly subjective and is very dependent on the teacher's grasp of the learner, the curriculum, pedagogy and learning theory. Some children can be overlooked unless the teacher is careful to observe quieter or less animated children.
Most recent summative data	Any data (reading scores, national test data, internal school data) that captures children's current attainment.	These sources can be very reliable as they are based on tests, often externally produced.	These sources can sometimes not provide a true, valid account of a learner's achievements and can be very narrow in focus. Tests are done at a fixed point in time and do not always allow learners to demonstrate their true potential.
Discussions with children/parents	Discussions (informal and formal) with the key participants (the children) and stakeholders (the parents) can help develop a full picture of learning and progress, providing information that is not captured anywhere else.	These discussions add a layer of insight. As professionals, we need to recognise that learners and parents are vital contributors to the assessment process.	The nature of the discussion, the questions asked and the context in which the discussions took place can influence the evidence captured. Parents may feel less confident in speaking to teachers. Children and parents may try to say what they think the teacher wants to hear.

There is no hierarchical order to the strategies suggested for obtaining initial assessment evidence in Table 5.1. The judicial use of these strategies will ensure that a valid context is created for designing and planning lessons that meet the needs of the learners and provide the best possible opportunities for all learners to make accelerated progress by pinpointing current understanding and building in an informed way from there. Amara's example from practice 5.2 puts some of these ideas into a practical classroom context. Amara came to the realisation that children need to understand a learning goal or objective and how to reach it if they are to achieve it (Sadler 1989).

Example from practice 5.2: Amara's planning for progress

Amara, a student teacher, began trialling a system of pre- and post-assessments in maths and English lessons to integrate self-assessment within them to help her to more effectively meet the specific needs of all learners.

The children were encouraged to attempt one question (a cold task or pre-assessment) before the teaching input and then complete a post-assessment question (hot task) following the lesson. Rather than focus on the activity, priority was given to the learning intention and how this learning would be best evidenced.

Amara's intentions were two-fold:

1　To enable the children to become more involved in evaluating their own progress and noticing their progress towards the learning objective. Children would be able to see for themselves whether they had made progress and could use this evidence to shape their efforts, focus their attention and articulate their learning journey.
2　To enable her, through observation and dialogue, to evaluate how successfully the children had engaged with the learning and gain evidence of the children's progress towards learning objectives. This would help to indicate what was needed next: whether that be further guidance and instruction, further opportunities for consolidation or a move towards more mastery aspects of the topic.

The pre-assessment was initially introduced by Amara modelling the thought processes involved when attempting something completely new or which appeared challenging. At the start of lessons she reminded the children about this with short encouraging prompts such as 'have a go' and 'it's okay if it's wrong, we haven't learnt it yet'.

At the end of the lesson and following their engagement with the learning opportunities, children completed the post-assessment question or task. Amara decided upon a system of sticky notes, which they used to record their self-assessment and stick in their exercise books. The children then placed their books into different piles depending upon how confident they felt that they had met the learning objective including a pile for children who felt they needed extra support, based upon their post-assessment question. This quickly helped identify learners for intervention support, greater encouragement, additional teacher attention, catch-up sessions or a pre-teach input prior to the next lesson. Once modelled and expectations made clear, this process became integral to the end of every lesson and all children were able to successfully self-assess their understanding and progress improved.

Throughout the process of trialling pre- and post-assessment, Amara found that planning within this cycle was hugely important because the pre- and post-assessment questions had to be precisely targeted to build from the previous post-assessment task. Amara reflected:

AfL should be recognised as central to classroom practice, it improves learning and informs teaching. By introducing pre and post assessment, even in the short term, every child would know how they're doing, what they need to do to improve and how to get there.

Rising to the challenges of assessment-informed planning

There are several potential challenges that may impact on a teacher's ability to effectively utilise assessment to inform planning. First, and potentially the most common, is the issue of time; just how do we fit in all of this assessment? The solution often lies within the teacher's capacity to multi-task. Effective practitioners will not need to spend a huge amount of time on 'additional assessment' as it will be embedded within their practice. In this sense, effective use of initial assessment to inform planning can be viewed as a low-cost, high-impact approach. We must recognise, appreciate and effectively utilise the vast mass of assessment evidence that we have available. This includes what is generated 'in the moment' and simply part of everyday good practice and rich learning. Within a lesson, a key challenge is how we create the capacity and thus use our professional 'eye' to be able to tune into and work with these valuable points in a lesson. Some researchers call these 'assessment conversations' (Serret, Correia & Harrison 2018). These are critical moments during a lesson where we might observe, notice, hear or be part of a discussion with children as they share, 'in the moment', what they might know, half know and don't know about a concept. This spontaneous evidence of learning, with judicious use of time, capacity and professional eye, can be the starting point for a mini-plenary during a lesson to move the learning forward for the whole class. This is formative assessment in action.

One of the other major challenges to achieving assessment-informed planning is the use of mass-produced schemes of planning for teachers. Whilst we should always be aiming to work in a way which is time efficient, there is a real danger that if we rely too heavily on such schemes then we will be neglecting to ensure that our planning is specific to the initial starting points of the children in our class or indeed ongoing assessment within the lesson. Just because we might be teaching a class a sequence of lessons on poetry does not necessarily dictate that a mass-produced scheme entitled 'Year x Poetry' is the most appropriate sequence of learning. Whilst this may well be a time-saving mechanism, we must always ensure that such schemes are personalised to support our own development of planning which must still directly be informed by our own assessment evidence.

It is clear that only when we as teachers know the exact starting points and current attainment for specific children and groups of children within our class then can we truly gauge how much progress they have made. If we only measure where they get to, this is not sufficient to build a clear case for how far they have come and how this was achieved. The most purposeful planning is that which begins with assessment and ensures it is assessment that drives the learning forwards.

Conclusion

In this chapter, planning for assessment is presented as something that is integrated and embedded within practice. Viewed as such, it allows us as teachers to capture evidence of learning before, during and after a lesson. Understanding that assessment serves a range of purposes and audiences is key. Our professional grasp of formative and summative assessment recognises this and can be a powerful professional tool, informing our pedagogical decisions when planning for assessment and learning. Finally, when planning for assessment, we need to involve the children so that they 'own their learning'. It is important that children can recognise their progress, articulate what they have learnt and identify their own next steps.

Points to ponder

How might our personal understanding of formative and summative assessment influence our day-to-day planning decisions?

What kind of learning environment is needed to promote autonomy so that children have the confidence, power and ability to articulate (and own) their learning journey?

Which assessment sources might be used more effectively and better support children's learning?

How can we embed assessment throughout the learning process so that it informs, develops and evaluates learning?

References

Black, P. & Wiliam, D. (1998) Assessment and classroom learning. *Assessment in Education: Principles Policy and Practice*, 5(1), 7–73.

Black, P. & Wiliam, D. (2018) Classroom assessment and pedagogy. *Assessment in Education: Principles, Policy & Practice*, 25(6), 551–575.

Dolin, J., Black, P., Harlen, W. & Tiberghien, A. (2018) Exploring relations between formative and summative assessment. In: Dolin, J. & Evans, R., eds., *Transforming assessment: Through an interplay between practice, research and policy*. Cham: Springer, 53–82.

Earle, S. (2017) The challenge of balancing key principles in teacher assessment. *Journal of Emergent Science*, 9(12), 41–47.

Harrison, C. & Howard, S. (2009) *Inside the primary black box: Assessment for learning in the classroom*. London: GLAssessment.

Naylor, S. & Keogh, B. (2000) *Concept cartoons in science education*. Stafford: Millgate House.

Sadler, D.R. (1989) Formative assessment and the design of instructional systems. *Instructional Science*, 18, 119–144.

Serret, N., Correia, C. & Harrison, C. (2018) Formative practice in primary science. In: Serret, N. & Earle, S. (eds.) *ASE guide to primary science education*, 4th ed. Hatfield: Association for Science Education, 2018, 116–124.

6

Questioning

Alison Murphy, Vicky McEwan and Catherine Gripton

Introduction

In this chapter, we explore questioning. We explain how important it is to plan teacher questions in advance and encourage children's questions through providing the right opportunities and environment. This chapter begins with the importance of questioning and types of questions that are asked in the classroom suggesting that fewer, more effective questions can be used by teachers where questions are *planned for* based upon the type of thinking we want to prompt from the children. It continues in considering how we can ensure that we really listen to and value children's questions. Towards the end of this chapter, there is an exploration of how teachers question children effectively for assessment, to prompt (higher order) thinking and to encourage children's questioning within a questioning-rich ethos and environment.

The importance of questioning

Questioning is fundamental to learning and teaching as a provocation or prompt for thinking (to support children to construct understanding). It is a powerful tool which requires careful planning (consideration before and within lessons or activities). We know that teacher questioning impacts upon children's achievement (Hattie 2003). Teachers and practitioners ask many questions everyday (sometimes as many as 400 according to Hastings 2003). It is important to recognise that all questions require something of a child. Questions, therefore, need to be purposeful and move learning forwards. Too many questions and the children experience overload: processing and constructing responses to an overwhelming number of prompts. Too few questions and children can become disengaged or learning can be superficial. Questions need to be authentic and well selected so that that learners see the need to formulate their own response. In Chapter 12, Gomersall and Gripton discuss, 'questions worth asking' which are genuine questions that are worthwhile to children. They argue that these types of questions are crucial to stimulate creative thinking.

The importance of answering

Children need to know how they are expected to answer questions posed by teachers and each other. As teachers, we need to make this explicit. Managing children's responses to our questions is key. Asking a single child to respond to a question posed is limiting as only one child's thinking is illuminated. This can lead to many children becoming disengaged. Going beyond a one-to-one answer helps us to better gauge the learning of all children through providing opportunities for everyone to respond to the question in a meaningful way. Examples of this include talk partners, thinking time and 'show me' activities (move, point, hold up, write, draw, select, mime). An emotionally safe learning environment is vital in order for children to feel able to share their thinking and trust that all ideas (even those not fully formed yet) are welcome and valued. Time is a crucial factor where children need time first to think and then to articulate or formulate their response.

Potential pitfalls in questioning include:

- Asking too many questions
- Giving insufficient thinking time
- Asking a question and answering it yourself
- Asking the quickest or highest attaining child
- Asking irrelevant or unnecessary questions (including using a question when it is actually an instruction, for example, 'Would you like to bring me your reading book?')
- Failing to follow up question responses (perhaps allowing misconceptions to go unchallenged)
- Asking a difficult question too early
- Asking too many of the same type of questions
- Making children uncomfortable with your questioning or asking questions in a threatening way (an interrogation)
- Asking questions which are not genuine (which we know the answer to)
- Never using probing questions which require deeper thinking
- Leaving children unclear on how you want them to respond
- Unnecessarily asking a question multiple times in different ways (rephrasing so that the children are busy processing language instead of considering the question)
- Asking questions buried within extended periods of teacher talk

Types of questions

Key questions are often included within planning formats and crucially are linked to the learning objective. *Key questions* support learning (as opposed to supplementary, non-essential questions or general questions for management or behaviour). Essential to planning effective questions is to think about the type of thinking that you want the children to engage in. *Closed questions* typically have only one answer and can be very useful to help children recall prior learning or known facts that they will need for a task. They can build children's confidence and create a buzz or energy within the classroom or setting. *Open questions* require children to create answers, perhaps more than one answer, and to explore. *Open questions* take much more time for children to respond to as they are constructing and reasoning. In answering *open questions*, our first response is rarely our best answer so by giving children time or asking them to generate more than one answer (perhaps in groups or using sticky notes) we are more likely to elicit their best thinking. We can also ask children to select their best answer from their multiple answers or to rank their answers (evaluation). This is supportive of using questions to encourage children to engage in thinking aloud (Gripton 2014) which makes their thinking more visible to other children (as a model) and to us as teachers for assessment.

Hinge questions (Wiliam 2005) are a formative assessment tool and a sophisticated way to use *multiple-choice questions* in order for the teacher to check children's understanding at a significant hinge point in the lesson. The children's responses indicate their current understanding and help the teacher to shape the next phase of the lesson. Understanding the content before the hinge point is a prerequisite for the next chunk of learning and knowledge of how the children have understood this is probed by the *hinge question*. Each multiple-choice answer must follow one (and only one) thought process so that the children's answers quickly reveal their thought processes to the teacher. The teacher (who knows which thought process leads to which answer) can then make teaching choices based upon this, perhaps providing alternative explanations or activities and delaying transition to the next phase of the lesson if necessary.

Deeper questioning

Some teachers plan questions in pairs or sequences so that the subsequent *follow-up questions* build upon the first and probe deeper thinking. Children can be asked to refine, expand upon or interrogate their own or another child's answer to give a deeper, more complete or conceptually bigger response. The teacher's response to the child's answer is important in supporting depth of thinking as a simple head nod, smile or 'tell me more' can be sufficient to prompt children to consider more fully, evaluate or contextualise their answer and offer additional insight. Sometimes known as '*popcorn' questioning*, the teacher does not always need to respond at all before another child. Children can nominate the next child to answer and a rapid series of answers can be quickly shared from a number of children. Whilst this does not necessarily promote deeper thinking, it does present a range of answers together which children can connect together to deepen their thinking. *Socratic questioning* is to systematically question to support deep conceptual critical thinking and question fundamental assumptions. It gets to the essence of an idea or concept by using challenging questions where the questioner (teacher or child) takes a naive position of knowing or assuming nothing so therefore questions everything, even accepted truths or knowledge. *Socratic questions* can be designed to clarify conceptual understanding, probe assumptions, interrogate reasoning, question viewpoints, probe implications and question the initial question itself (requiring a defence of its relevance or importance). Socratic questioning requires time and a supportive environment where children perceive this challenge as supportive of their learning. Questions can be scaffolded (more substantial initial support but then reduced) and sequenced so that children are eased gently into this challenge and heightened levels of critical thinking.

Questions to challenge thinking

Through planning questions purposefully and carefully (using knowledge of the range of questions that can be used and the type of thinking they will prompt) teachers can aim to ask fewer but crucially more effective questions. Table 6.1 provides types of questions and examples of how these can be worded to lead to the particular type of thinking that we would like from the children. Clearly, we need a varied approach in line with the stage of the lesson or activity to ensure that we are asking the right questions at the right time in order to move learning forwards. As children experience different types of questions in school, they become accustomed to the type of thinking expected of them and begin to anticipate questions, starting to formulate responses to questions not even asked yet which creates a culture of questioning and inquisitiveness in the classroom or setting.

Progressive questioning can be planned so that the question sequence supports progression in learning. Questions can be planned which move the children's thinking from simple to complex and structured to open-ended. Across the sequence of questions, decisions and solutions can increasingly become the child's responsibility as the lesson progresses.

Listening to and valuing children's questions

Children ask questions from an early age, and for many, these are initially spontaneous, casual comments about everyday observations that they are seeking clarification about. Statements such as 'Doggy Bark?' seek affirmation and clarification and gradually move to seeking explanations to help them find out more. Thus, the observation about the dog barking may turn into a question 'Why doggy barking?' These spontaneous casual questions emerge in children's everyday routines and conversations, and it is through these questions, children develop casual theories about their world that will evolve and change overtime. Leng Chua, Tan and Sock Wah Chng (2017) highlight to us the importance of mediated interactions between the child and their environment with the adult acting as a facilitator asking questions to enhance cognitive development.

Tizard and Hughes (1984) found that children asked far fewer questions at school than home and that at school children tended to answer rather than ask. This finding prompts us to question why. Why do children stop this natural curiosity about their world once they enter the school system? This natural curiosity about their world is nurtured in the home environment and in their everyday relationships with family and people they know well. When parents value, respond and help them to make sense of their questions children begin to refine their thinking, developing new

TABLE 6.1 Example questions to promote thinking

Questions about...	Thinking prompted...	Examples in context				
		Reading comprehension (English)	Repeating pattern (mathematics)	Living Processes – Fruit (Science)	Fine art (art and design)	Exploring an artefact (history)
Knowledge	Recall	What is this character called?	What comes after elephant in the pattern?	What is this fruit called?	Who is the artist?	Is it a clay pipe?
Evidence	Analysis	How do you know that the bear is cross?	How do you know that the next animal is an elephant?	Why do some fruits have more than one seed?	How do you know that the painting is of something important?	How do you know that it is a particularly old clay pipe?
Connection	Synthesis or evaluation	Is the dog a good friend?	Which bit repeats over and over?	Once planted, can you predict what will be needed for germination? ...and growth?	What do you like about the painting?	How is it similar or different to the other clay pipes found here?
Reasoning	Argument	Why was the boy worried?	Why is the elephant always next to the giraffe?	Why are fruits important?	Why did the artist use so much white paint?	Why is the pipe in this river bed?
Hypothetical	Counterfactual	What would have happened if the dog had not found the bear?	What would we do to keep a repeating pattern if I added a penguin to the beginning?	How do we know that a carrot is not a fruit?	How would the painting be different if the ship was in the centre?	If it was a more modern pipe, what size would it be and what would it be made out of?
	Creative and convergent	What do you think that they will do on the next day?	What would the 100th animal be?	If you discovered a new fruit in the rainforest, what might it be like?	If you were to add more of one colour, what would it be and why?	Who might have owned this pipe?
	Creative and divergent	What could happen on another day out?	What other patterns could I make?	What other factors influence the life cycle of a plant?	If you could commission a painting by this artist, what would you ask them to paint?	What other artefacts from the same time period might be found here?

(Adapted from Taggart et al. 2005).

theories. As they move into more formalised care settings the shift often changes and children find themselves in environments where they no longer have available adults to respond to them or the time and space to allow themselves to pause, ponder and wallow in their questions.

Children ask questions to help them to make meaning of their worlds. Children's questions are therefore a window to their emerging theories (Callanan & Oakes 1992), and by listening and responding teachers can illuminate misconceptions, identify next steps and support children to go further with their thinking. We will now explore how teachers from the early years and through primary can create an environment where children are allowed and encouraged to question and how teachers can support children's learning in all areas of the curriculum by listening to the questions they ask. Callanan and Oakes (1992) found that pre-school children were formulating sophisticated and often complex questions to acquire specific information about things that have puzzled them in their world. In this next example from practice 6.1 we will see a child create a context by her questions for the adults, both parents and teachers, to build upon.

Example from practice 6.1: Poppy's questions

Poppy is a three-year-old who attended nursery for five sessions a week. Poppy had just experienced the death of a beloved family pet and needed to ask a lot of questions to help her understand what had happened. The family pet had been buried in the garden, and her questions emerged about this as she asked 'Will Izzie be cold outside?', 'Izzie didn't like the rain, will she need an umbrella, can we see what the weather will be like for her?', 'When is Izzie coming back inside?', 'What can Izzie eat underground, I don't think she likes mud very much?'. Her questions were posed both at nursery and home as she tried to make sense of what happened. Nursery and home discussed how they would approach her questions and decided to use clear and factual information. The staff at nursery listened to Poppy and shared their experiences of a dog dying. They valued her questions, acknowledged her feelings and gave her the words to begin to make sense of what had happened.

This example illustrates the need to value and listen to children and the things that are important to them. In this case it helped the child cope emotionally but also through the questions, topics such as life and death, the weather and decay emerged and were explored. She drew pictures and shared stories about her dog's life developing her language, communication and literacy. The learning was rich and beyond the realms of most three-year olds' nursery topics, but it was relevant to Poppy. It mattered to her. Consider the factors that supported this.

First, the staff were brave in helping Poppy to answer her questions. They did not shy away from dealing with a difficult topic but tackled it head on. They took risks in sharing their own experiences of death and how they felt. They explained to other parents why they were talking about it and why it was necessary.

Second, the staff worked with the family. The dialogue we have with children enables us to listen to children effectively. We see the child in the context of not only the school or setting environment but their home and community. As teachers, we need to recognise the expertise parents have in understanding their children's learning processes. In order to capture this expertise, we need to recognise the importance of reciprocity in our interactions with parents about children's learning. Children will revisit their working theory as they grapple with a new concept. They will question, unpick, rebuild and construct new meaning through their questioning not only at school but in the home, and by working together we will support these cognitive processes.

Third, they did not allow themselves to be constrained by the curriculum or pre-set topics but were confident to move with the pace of the children, to allow the children and their questions to identify the possibilities for learning. The asking of questions identifies to us that a child has a gap in their knowledge and that they need to find answers to resolve this. They look towards more knowledgeable others to scaffold their learning (Vygotsky 1978) and to help answer the question. Finally, they respected the child's right to ask a question and they valued her questions.

Creating the environment for children to question also includes ensuring that children from the early years and through primary have the opportunity to pause, ponder and wallow in their learning, their thinking and their questioning. Providing experiences that will help them to develop awe and wonder in their world will hook them into things that excite and ignite their curiosity.

Reflection on questioning

When considering children's questions, we need to use a reflective lens and role model reflection on their questions. We can develop this through talking to children about the questions they ask and encouraging them to go deeper with a line of questioning. Can they apply the question they have asked to other things? What links can they follow? Where did their question lead them? What do they now know? What new thinking have they arrived at? This requires a skilful practitioner who is able to provide both autonomy for children to think, question and discover for themselves and stimulation through effective questioning (McEwan 2016).

This discussion with children about their questioning can illuminate learning and help us to become better at questioning. This requires responding to the child in the moment and goes beyond designing questions to check knowledge. Engaging curiosity and enabling children to see the learning through new eyes can be done through higher order questioning and skilful management.

As with Poppy, in the earlier example, provocations that arise from everyday contexts stimulate children's thinking and prompt them to ask and answer their own questions. Problems or situations, such as those provided by concept cartoons (Keogh & Naylor 1999), can represent alternative understandings as well as unearthing common misconceptions by children (see Chapter 5). The problems explored seek to make the familiar strange and the strange familiar. They are an indirect way of questioning the children's thinking and reasoning. They support the teacher to gain feedback and to address the misconceptions revealed. In the course of debating their ideas, children have the opportunity to engage in interactive, dialogic talk in groups and sustained shared thinking where they articulate their thoughts, question each other, propose explanation or justify reasoning (Driver, Newton & Osborne 2000). These mediated learning experiences (Leng Chua, Tan & Sock Wah Chng 2017) encourage active involvement and reflection on learning and therefore have the potential to create a shift in conceptual thinking.

Empowering children to question and embedding this as a feature of our every-day classroom interactions establishes positive learning dispositions such as curiosity and taking responsibility as well as promoting early critical thinking. It recognises children as engaged, invested, autonomous learners. Valuing children's questions encourages children to move beyond what they already know and personalises learning, making it meaningful for each individual. The questions that children ask provide us with vital assessment information as it reveals aspects of what they have understood. Children's questions can also be an important starting point for planning, helping teachers to tailor the planning to the needs and interests of the children and to avoid assumptions about what the children already know. Children's questions are as important as teacher's questions, and both are essential to consider within effective planning for learning.

Points to ponder

What type of thinking do you want the children to engage in and therefore what type of question do you need to pose?

Which types of question do you use most/least often? (This could be a good focus for an observation of your practice)

Do you fall into any of the questioning 'common pitfalls' identified in this chapter?

Is it always made explicit to children how they are expected to respond to a teacher question (for example, thinking time, paired discussion, show me, hand up, indicate, mime, point and all respond)?

References

Callanan, M. & Oakes, L. (1992) Pre-schoolers' questions and parents' explanations: Casual thinking in everyday activities. *Cognitive Development*, 7(2), 213–233.

Driver, R., Newton, P. & Osborne, J. (2000) Establishing the norms of scientific argumentation in classrooms. *Science Education*, 84(3), 287–312.

Gripton, C. (2014) Playing with thinking. In: Woods, A., ed., *The characteristics of effective learning: Creating and capturing the possibilities in the early years*. London: Routledge,2014, 71–86.

Hastings, S. (2003) Questioning. *Times Educational Supplement*, 04 July, 13.

Hattie, J. (2003) Teachers make a difference, what is the research evidence? Available at: https://research.acer.edu.au/research_conference_2003/4

Keogh, B. & Naylor, S. (1999) Concept cartoons, teaching and learning in science: An evaluation. *International Journal of Science Education*, 21(4), 431–446.

Leng Chua, B., Tan, O. & Sock Wah Chng, P. (2017) Mediated learning experience: Questions to enhance cognitive development of young children. *Journal of Cognitive Education and Psychology*, 16(2), 178–192.

McEwan, V. (2016) The role of practitioner involvement in supporting children's involvement. In: Woods, A., ed., *Examining levels of involvement in the early years: Engaging with children's possibilities*. Oxon: Routledge, 75–90.

Taggart, G., Ridley, K., Rudd, P. & Benefield, P. (2005) *Thinking skills in the early years: A literature review*. Berkshire: National Foundation for Educational Research.

Tizard, B. & Hughes, M. (1984) *Young children learning*. Cambridge MA: Harvard University Press.

Vygotsky, L. S. (1978) *Mind in society: The development of higher psychological processes*. Cambridge, MA: Harvard University Press.

Wiliam, D. (2005) Keeping learning on track: Formative assessment and the regulation of learning. In Coupland, M., Anderson, J. & Spencer T., Eds., *Making mathematics vital: Proceedings of the twentieth biennial conference of the Australian Association of Mathematics Teachers*. Adelaide: Australian Association of Mathematics Teachers, 26–40.

7

Planning for learners of English as an additional language

Nicky-Jane Kerr-Gilbert

Introduction

In this chapter, we consider what 'English as an Additional Language' (EAL) means for children and their teachers. We explore the complexities and variation within this and consider the impact on the child at different stages of language acquisition. The chapter seeks to support and develop practice by suggesting research-informed approaches and classroom strategies to base planning on, and also to provoke reflective thinking and develop the educational philosophy of inclusive teachers. We draw on the voices and experiences of student teachers whilst planning to support learners for whom English is an additional language.

What does EAL mean?

First, we must emphasise the value to children and teachers of living and learning in our increasingly diverse school communities as societies engage in global travel and migration. School census data informs us that the UK is a super diverse society with the number of children learning EAL rising steadily. There are over 300 languages spoken in primary schools in England, for example, where approximately one in five (over 1 million) children is a learner of EAL (DfE 2019). Chapter 3 promotes the importance of an inclusive environment where trends over time evidence that our children are learning in and benefitting from a fast changing global landscape of diversity.

Confusion may develop from the umbrella term of 'EAL' that can mean so many different things. For some teachers, adaptation to planning and provision will be minimal as children identified as learners of English as an additional language are assessed to be very proficient in reading, writing, speaking and listening in English; many being second- and third-generation English language learners. However, sometimes teachers will need to rapidly respond to be able to support a child who is not only new to English but also may be new to formal schooling. In the case of asylum seekers or refugee families, a child may be experiencing real anxiety due to displacement in addition to learning EAL. Assessment of a child in challenging circumstances such as these can be difficult for a teacher, requiring patience and understanding as children might not be able to show all that they know on the first day in their new school. Recent arrivals to the UK may be highly proficient in their first language but can experience isolation in a new primary school setting when the people, language and school systems are unfamiliar. Some children may not yet be proficient in their first language, and their needs will be clearly different to a child with high levels of language proficiency.

Not all children deemed new arrivals will be staying permanently in the UK. Sojourners may be children attending UK schools for short periods of time while parents work or study. Some of these children may benefit from being multi-literate learners who read, write and speak proficiently in a range of languages and may have inbuilt family or community language support. Clearly, the group of learners for which we use the term EAL is highly diverse, and therefore, we need to be sufficiently skilled as teachers to plan purposefully for each of these children in order for them to learn effectively.

Bilingualism roughly translates as 'living in two languages'; this means that language is inextricably linked to social and cultural identity. The barriers experienced when learning a second language may affect the child's sense of identity and self-esteem. Some educators consider the use of a first language as 'language interference' and believe that languages should be kept separate in the classroom (perceiving language diversity as a problem). This may result in the child being instructed to speak only in English at school, resulting in a devaluing of their home language and potentially their home culture, values, beliefs and even faith. Some teachers approach language development with a belief that children will 'pick up' English naturally when immersed in English-speaking environments and that there are 'critical periods' beyond which developing a second language will be more difficult. Both of these beliefs are unhelpful to teachers as they suggest that we do not need to plan specifically for individual children with English as an additional language.

Cummins' (2000) well-established model of acquiring English as an additional language describes the interrelated factors that affect learning. This model makes it clear that learners' social and cultural experiences will have an impact on their progress in language acquisition as well as on their cognitive and academic development. It is a positive model for education as it suggests that teachers can actively and effectively support children for whom English is an additional language. Hazel's experiences as a student teacher demonstrate the practical application of this model to practice (examples from practice 7.1, 7.2 and 7.3). Example from practice 7.1 shows the positive impact that Hazel's application of the Cummins model had upon both her and Gabriel, a child in her placement class. Hazel recognised that the positive relationship she fostered was key to the development of Gabriel's confidence and enthusiasm. Hazel recognised the importance of valuing links with families, reflecting the significance of respecting the role of the family in supporting the child.

Example from practice 7.1: Hazel develops her relationship with Gabriel

Hazel, a student teacher on her final placement, excitedly emailed her tutor.

'Just wanted to share some progress I have had in school with the child who is learning EAL that we spoke about. I have given him some Romanian/English cards for him to carry around with pictures for basic classroom routines, as well as sending an English/Romanian activity book home with a letter to his parents in Romanian. It seems they feel really happy about all of this and myself and Gabriel have developed a good relationship in which he seems to trust me. The results have been great. Attached you will find a picture of Gabriel's first piece of independent work he's ever done since starting school – I only wish you could see his smile! As well as this, in my French lesson today, he put up his hand to answer a question for the first time, which is massive considering his previous hesitation to get involved. I genuinely feel like he's so much happier already, and to me, that is the most important thing. Next steps will be developing his learning, and trying to get him more confident in his own abilities'.

Cummins (2000) suggests that children first acquire Basic Interpersonal Communicative Skills (BICS) where everyday vocabulary and informal language used face to face is context embedded – supported by external contextual cues and is used to narrate, describe, name and compare. Cognitive and Academic Language Proficiency (CALP) develops over a longer period of time where a full range of vocabulary and formal language will be used for a range of purposes independently of contextual cues. Cummins (2000) suggests that those who have developed CALP in their first language are more likely to be able to transfer this learning to acquisition of additional languages for cognitively demanding language tasks. The implication of this is that we need to recognise the changes that a child will experience in their English language development over time. The model also encourages teachers to consider the benefits of transfer from a first language to a second and to value opportunities where children are enabled to think, talk, plan, read or write in a first language to support their development of language.

When we plan for children for whom English is an additional language, it is useful to consider three phases of support – before new learning, during new learning and after new learning – to help us understand our role in assessing, planning, teaching, intervening and evaluating impact effectively to support their progress as learners.

Before new learning

Before learning we know that a child needs to feel their basic needs have been met, this involves developing good relationships, enabling learners to feel safe in a new environment, valuing individuals and promoting self-esteem. As teachers, we are mindful of Maslow's (1943) hierarchy of needs and the importance of developing a sense of belonging to enable self-motivated learning. Therefore, it is important for teachers to learn about the child in order to sow the seeds of belonging but also crucially to know about the culture of the child so we can develop the learning environment and select resources to challenge prejudice. The second comment from Hazel (example from practice 7.2) exemplifies how she is learning about the importance of engaging with the child's prior experiences as a beginning teacher.

Example from practice 7.2: Hazel learns more about Gabriel

Having emailed her tutor the week before, Hazel (student teacher) contacted her tutor again.

'As well as gaining confidence around the classroom and a general happiness, I have found out that Gabriel cannot read Romanian or English because in Romania children don't go to school until they're 7, I believe? However, I have started a daily intervention of phase 2 phonics. Slow progress but it is a start! His maths is strong if visual so that's good. I'm just glad he's started to gain more confidence around school'.

Induction processes are an important initial starting point to enable us to build up a profile of the child. One strategy is to develop passports to the classroom/school emphasising important initial words and phrases such as people and places, practical needs and common queries (for example, 'When is my mum coming back?'). Another strategy is to buddy the child up with a good English language role model, sometimes this could be a child who shares the same first language. Accessing translators, dual language resources, home language resources through the family, community organisations or dual language dictionaries supports practitioners in developing displays and classroom labels as well as providing teachers with knowledge of some basic instructions and words of praise in the child's first language. Pre-teaching or flipped learning strategies can be very valuable in preparing the child for new learning. These strategies involve preparing a child in a timely way before new learning is introduced in order to develop their confidence and ensure they are more readily able to access new learning. If family members also speak English, they may be able to support pre-teaching experiences in a safe environment at home using dual language texts or acting as interpreters to pre-teach key vocabulary or ideas.

Non-verbal communication including facial expression and gesture, alongside repetition of key vocabulary using embedded contextual cues, should be used to support clear language in modelling, questioning and instructing. Continuing with Hazel's practice (example from practice 7.3), she recognised the impact of non-verbal communication and found that her modelling of these had supported the child's ability to communicate independently. Her modelling also supported the development of relationships with other children so that Gabriel became included in the learning community in the classroom.

Example from practice 7.3: Hazel communicates effectively with Gabriel

Hazel updated her tutor about what she is learning from working with Gabriel.

'Facial expression is a massive thing I have found, and little actions! Creating the basic language cards also help him access the classroom – despite him not being able to read them, the visual helps and he can show me what he needs/how he feels.

I find it also helps me! Because there is Romanian on them, I can speak the Romanian that he recognises. The children are also really warming to him, which is lovely. Lots of new friendships are being made. I think they bounce off one another and I notice he is picking up a lot of English phrases'.

Involving carers and families in the child's learning journey can have very positive outcomes for the child. Teachers often develop a family box, a culture basket or a display area where every child has the opportunity to bring in objects and artefacts from home to show or share with the class. Teachers often do this informally with younger children and more formally with older children to promote an appreciation of cultural diversity. These help a child feel valued in the classroom, support peer relationships and lay solid foundations for new learning.

During new learning

During learning, interactive teaching and multimodal texts are important elements of effective teaching. Multimodal texts communicate meaning in different modes or methods, including, for example, visual still or moving images in film or picture books, alongside music and sound in film or layout and presentation of the written word in texts such as graphic novels or comics where colour, font size style and direction may support interpreting the meaning of the text. For a child who is proficient in their first language, we should encourage reading and writing in their first language. Explicit modelling and use of guided experiences of reading and writing partners to develop collaborative learning are good quality teaching strategies. As teachers, we need to provide real purposes for reading and writing that are based on real experiences, and this should include an understanding of the child's previous life and learning. For example, a student teacher planned maths problems based on money as she realised that this was something that the children had real experiences of outside school. The familiar experience supported application of new learning in a practical context. New learning is built on the foundations of previous learning in order for children to construct new knowledge (Piaget 1926).

Scaffolding and structure are the cornerstones of effective planning, and this is particularly important for children learning EAL where teacher modelling and emphasis are based upon knowledge of the child's needs. Group and independent activities can be planned to build specifically on the new skills that we have modelled in order to provide sufficient scaffolding for the child. To support development of self-esteem, groupings need to be considered carefully. If a specific educational need has been identified for the child then it may sometimes be deemed appropriate to group the child with learners with similar needs. We need to be very wary, however, of grouping children learning EAL with children identified as having special educational needs or disabilities or children identified as having lower levels of attainment unless there is a specific reason to do so (based on careful assessment). Learners of EAL have very different needs, and grouping them together based purely on the EAL label may isolate the children, stigmatise them and ultimately not meet their learning needs. A more inclusive approach may work better to meet the child's need for purposeful interaction with strong English language models.

Purposeful planning includes how we use appropriate resources, and these are vital for children learning EAL. Visual resources and graphic organisers (such as talking, writing and thinking frames) can support the language demands of activities so that the child can focus their attention on the new learning. Technology can be used to scaffold and reinforce new vocabulary and ideas. Dictogloss, for example, is an activity where the teacher reads/dictates a text that learners then reconstruct by listening and noting down key words. The text may be read several times to allow children to build up a bank of key vocabulary to support reconstruction. In addition to new curricular learning, all children should experience a range of opportunities to develop language and social skills. Games are a good way to do this. Barrier games, for example, are two player games where a physical barrier is present between players, or where children sit back to back. The barrier encourages them to verbally share information, explain or discuss in a playful way.

The importance of feedback cannot be underestimated for children learning EAL. Feedback needs to be frequent and communicated clearly, considering the child's proficiency in English. Specific positive praise, reinforcing where the child has been successful, is motivating. Providing models and examples can be particularly helpful for children to gain a clear understanding of what is being asked of them. Using good examples or WAGOLLs (what a good one looks like) and poor examples or WABOLLs (what a bad one looks like) to teach through misconceptions is good practice. Using 'show me', 'improve it', 'prove it' or 'explain it' approaches to encourage children to use language to explain, expand and reason supports self-editing, awareness of mistakes and understanding of success criteria. Good quality first teaching strategies include setting targets through visual, oral and written feedback to support the learner. As teachers, we need to assess spoken and written language development. This includes looking for particular errors that children learning EAL might commonly make in use of tense, determiners and pronouns when working in English.

If assessment (see Chapter 5) identifies that a child learning EAL is yet to develop the vocabulary to narrate or explain, teachers need to plan opportunities for vocabulary development to ensure children are not language impoverished. In planning for shared and guided reading, the focus needs to be on comprehension not just decoding and word reading. In planning, we need to consider the teaching of new vocabulary using additional resources or pre-teaching for definitions to make reading sessions meaningful for children who are developing their English vocabulary. There are many websites that provide visual and audio stories for learners to watch or listen to at home or school to prepare for or follow up reading sessions. Some books have QR codes that enable children to listen along to the story being read while turning the pages, and we can create our own QR codes taping children and adults reading stories in a range of languages to make personalised provision. Subject-specific vocabulary support can help children in mathematics and science lessons, for example, where vocabulary posters, books and digital resources can support the learning.

Some approaches to supporting learners of EAL are fundamental regardless of the stage of language acquisition. All children need to hear words in many contexts before they become embedded. It is important that we encourage all adults working in a setting to model Standard English. We also need to be explicit in unpicking idioms and examples of colloquial language to support the child's understanding. Encounters with words need to be memorable, and very often we need to consider compensatory experiences to provide additional and necessary contextual information to support learning, such as the use of artefacts, objects, pictures, video, story, role-play and experiential learning. This was recognised by Sasha, a student teacher early in her initial teacher education, who came to the realisation that 'most conversations have to be supported with visuals' and this mantra can guide us to have more effective classroom communication.

In planning, it can be helpful to consider Gibbons' (2015) idea of an 'information backlog' for learners where the pace of learning may be too fast for a new language learner. We need to consider whether some children are always several steps behind, trying to translate and understand contextual information before taking on board instructions to complete a task. This indicates that the pace of learning may need adapting for these learners, repetition may support understanding and contextual cues are vital. If children are transcribing from one language to another or translating in their head as they read, appropriate time needs to be given to support these processes and children may need to make notes or jottings. Where strategies such as 'word of the day' are used to develop vocabulary for the class, we may add to this by developing personalised word of the day images and lists for individual children. This works particularly well and supports self-esteem by making this reciprocal – so a learner of EAL may introduce a word of the day in their first language to the rest of the class.

After new learning

To follow up new learning, lots of experience to apply it needs to be provided for all children but this is particularly the case for children for whom English is an additional language. This may be through play or experiential learning opportunities but could also be discrete follow-up sessions with additional adults in small groups or homework tasks that provide further practice. Liaising with families and carers to support the child in engaging meaningfully and authentically with new learning is part of encouraging a true home-school partnership where carers and educators share common goals and approaches to support the child. Examples of this include providing photocopies or photographs of a child's work to take home for revisiting and sharing or providing copies of class texts for home use.

Assessment

Throughout planning for children learning EAL, continual assessment is key. Initial and ongoing assessment of the child's English language development as well as curriculum learning is necessary to target planning and support for their individual needs. The Department for Education (DfE) in England used A-E codes between 2016 and 2018 to support a requirement to report proficiency and progress in English for learners of EAL. Although no longer required by government, these provide us with a good starting point for assessing individual children and informing teacher planning. Useful resources to support the codes to assess pupils learning

EAL are provided by the Bell Foundation (2017) in listening, speaking, reading and viewing, and in writing. Using these A–E assessment codes, we can plan to incorporate specific strategies in our lessons to support individual children at differing levels of English proficiency. Continuing this assessment in an ongoing way supports the regular setting of new targets for the child and continued planning for opportunities for language development to support the child to become more proficient in English (moving through these stages).

Conclusion

As 21st-century teachers we are preparing young learners for the future, and it is, therefore, up to us to sow the seeds which will enable children to fully engage in future society. Language and communication are key factors contributing to a child's success in developing independence in their social and academic development. Working with children for whom English is an additional language is as much about our own educational philosophy as about strategies and resources. It is about a commitment to supporting every learner to fulfil their potential. We therefore need to continually reflect upon our approach to planning for children learning EAL. We need to question what we see and reflect on how we can help each child to develop and learn more effectively. There are plenty of differing practices in our schools and plenty of resources available to access but we need to be guided by a sense of our own philosophy so that we are able to look for resources and strategies that match our own thinking, rather than picking an 'off the shelf' generic resource. As teachers, we adapt to meet the needs of individual learners; we innovate and create to do our very best for the children.

Points to ponder

What are your beliefs about how children will become proficient in English and what impact might this have upon a child?

How will you develop a strong relationship with a child when you do not speak the same language yet? What do you need to know about the background, culture, experiences and interests of the child to plan effectively?

What resources will you use to support an individual child learning EAL? How will you ensure that there are visual and other prompts to support dialogue?

How will you involve families and carers as learning partners?

What assessment framework will you employ to assess English language proficiency and how will you adapt your planning accordingly?

What 'before, during and after' strategies will support your planning for children learning English as an Additional Language

References

Bell Foundation. (2017) *EAL assessment framework* [online]. Available at: www.bell-foundation.org.uk/eal-programme/teaching-resources/eal-assessment-framework/

Cummins, J. (2000) *Language, power and pedagogy: Bilingual children in the crossfire*. Clevedon: Multilingual Matters.

Department for Education [DfE]. (2019) *Schools, pupils and their characteristics: January 2018* [online]. Available at: https://assets.publishing.service.gov.uk/government/uploads/system/uploads/attachment_data/file/812539/Schools_Pupils_and_their_Characteristics_2019_Main_Text.pdf

Gibbons, P. (2015) *Scaffolding language, scaffolding learning: Teaching English language learners in the mainstream classroom.* Portsmouth: Heinemann.

Maslow, A. H. (1943) A theory of human motivation. *Psychological Review,* 50(4), 370–396.

Piaget, J. (1926) *The language and thought of the child.* New York: Harcourt Brace & Company.

8

Planning for children's needs

Steven Sharp, Clare Orridge and Richard Muge

Introduction

This chapter examines the overall ethos underpinning the field of Special Educational Needs education and ideas for enabling learning with specific emphasis on communication, socialisation, attention and self-esteem. In planning for children with needs, we recognise that aspects of good practice benefit every child, and as teachers we adapt and develop our practice to meet the needs of all the children in our setting. However, there are some children with additional needs for whom we need to pay particular attention to in our planning. These children may or may not have an identified Special Educational Need and Disability (SEND).

What is SEND?

The following formal definition is extracted from the English SEND Code of Practice, Department for Education and Department of Health (2015).

> *A child or young person has SEND if he or she has a significantly greater difficulty in learning than the majority of others of the same age, or has a disability which prevents or hinders him or her from making use of facilities of a kind generally provided for others of the same age in mainstream schools or mainstream post-16 institutions.*

Whilst different countries have different definitions and descriptions for special educational needs, the term generally refers to learners who experience difficulties that make it harder for them to achieve their learning potential than most children and young people of the same age.

How is a child identified as having a particular need?

Approaches for identifying a range of needs vary across different education systems. In 2011 the DAFFODIL (**Dynamic Assessment of Functioning Oriented at**

Development and Inclusive Learning) project, was created by a consortium of eight European partners in order to research more inclusive alternatives and suggest reforms to assessment and coaching procedures (Lebeer et al. 2011). This was the beginning of a unified practice arrangement for a standardised set of descriptions, psychometric tests and mechanisms for teaching.

In identifying SEND, labels are commonly used. At this point it is interesting to examine our own thoughts with regard to whether the allocation of a label of need is necessary. Some countries define only one or two types of special needs (for example, Denmark). Others categorise pupils with special needs in more than ten categories (Poland). Most countries distinguish 6–10 types of special needs. In Liechtenstein, no types of special needs are distinguished; only the type of support is defined (Education, Audiovisual and Culture Executive Agency 2010). As teachers we plan for meeting children's needs, regardless of labels used within settings and educational systems.

Example from practice 8.1: Student teachers discuss the value of labels

A group of student teachers were discussing two contrasting perspectives on the value of labels in education. On one side, Oli and Jaspreet argued that any need identified might lead to a 'self-fulfilling prophecy' where a child will live up to the expectation of the teacher, so could led to low expectations. They cited Carol Dweck's work on mindsets as a potential indicator that the teacher's mindset may influence the children.

On the other side of the argument, Lauren and Alex took a more pragmatic perspective in that a label helps to increase the awareness of the need and focus the attention of busy teachers onto realistic learning opportunities. They also pointed out that additional funding can be linked to labels.

The students debated this for some time and could all see the merits of both sides of the argument.

The quandary that the student teachers in the example from practice 8.1 were wrestling with is something that is a common concern for most teachers. Experienced teachers are often grateful of additional, more expert, support when teaching children who may have more complex requirements. This leaves something of a dichotomy, with the granting of a label fulfilling a practical need but at the same time, a sincere belief that the system in use in Lichtenstein (where only the type of support is defined and needs are not labelled) is a useful aspirational model. Although it is highly likely that we, as professionals, will all have our own thoughts and experiences with regard to these considerations, the fact that we spend a few moments in contemplation of the issue is, perhaps, healthy.

How do we adapt our planning to accommodate children's individual needs?

Teachers should meet the diverse needs of all children, not simply those identified with SEND, by adopting a variety of approaches to learning, teaching and assessment (Vickerman 2007). Planning for children's needs requires a detailed understanding of the child: what they excel at; what they struggle with, the size of any attainment gap with their peers; who they work well with; and who they don't. We differentiate to provide equity in learning and to redress the imbalance of opportunity experienced by some children.

How can we do this?

Always with an eye on equity and closing attainment gaps or helping children fulfil their potential, we need to consider:

- What will I teach?
  - Do we teach the same to all?
  - Is the content pitched correctly?
  - Is it relevant to the child?
- How will I teach?
  - How does the child or children learn best?
  - How will we engage and interest children?
  - How do we enable children to be autonomous learners?
- What scaffolding will be most effective?
  - How much scaffolding will provide for progress but enable children to become independent learners?
- Who is best equipped to provide scaffolding and enable learning?
  - How can all adults be planned for to work effectively?
  - Will the children with the most complex needs be taught by the teacher?
  - How will children support each other effectively?

Within our planning we need to differentiate appropriately to meet the needs of all learners. There are many models of differentiation, but the foundations of most are based on the following precepts (see Table 8.1).

In planning for differentiation, taking account of the aspects of the PACIER model in Table 8.1, we can plan for the needs of all children including those with

TABLE 8.1 PACIER model for differentiation

Precise	Personalised needs are planned for based upon detailed knowledge of the individual child
Aspirational	High expectations for all children regardless of the need
Consistent	Across subjects and contexts
Inclusive	For all children
Engaging	Relevant, meaningful and purposeful for the child
Responsive	Flexible to changing needs and emerging assessment

additional needs. However to fully meet the more complex needs of some children we should carefully consider the nature of their additional needs and plan for these explicitly.

Identification of additional needs

Recognising that the categories of need in use in the UK are not necessarily shared by other countries, it makes sense to adopt an approach suggested by the OECD (a conglomerate of 22 countries) using a three-category framework (Table 8.2):

The needs of children within Categories B and C may also be found within the more complex needs of children in Category A. The following sections explore aspects of practice for the most common needs. Although these may be described using different terminology in different settings, we consider communication (Category C), socialisation, self-esteem and attention (Category B). The examination of these categories of need matches closely with the most common needs identified for the UK, namely, MLD (Moderate Learning Difficulties), SEMH (Social, Emotional and Mental Health) and S&L (Speech and Language).

Communication needs

Difficulties with communication often form part of the additional needs that children experience in schools. These can vary from mild pronunciation difficulties to alternatives forms of communication, such as augmentative communication. Communication is more than just speech. Every day we use a range of non-verbal gestures and facial expressions to convey meaning. We also use sounds, written symbols and other visuals in a range of ways to communicate our thoughts, feelings and needs. The communication difficulties which teachers support in schools are wide and varied, with one in ten children having a speech, language or communication need (The Communication Trust 2014).

Children may have difficulty articulating, distinguishing between or combining speech sounds, resulting in unclear speech. They may struggle to join words together into sentences to make themselves understood, or there may be difficulties in understanding and processing the language of others. Understanding how gestures, facial expressions and language are combined to demonstrate another's intention

TABLE 8.2 OECD Tri-Partite System for categorising students (2007)

Category A: disabilities with organic origins where there is substantial normative agreement about the categories (for example, sensory, motor, severe and profound intellectual disabilities).

Category B: difficulties that do not appear to have organic origins or be directly linked to socio-economic, cultural or linguistic factors (for example, behavioural difficulties, mild learning difficulties, specific learning difficulties and dyslexia).

Category C: difficulties that arise from socio-economic, cultural and/or linguistic factors; some disadvantaged or atypical background that education seeks to compensate for.

or point of view may also be challenging for individuals. For some children their Speech, Language and Communication Need (SLCN) is the only difficulty they have, but for others, it may be part of another condition, such as autism or a hearing impairment. Children with less severe SLCN may seem more immature in their development than their peers, but it is important to recognise that having more limited verbal communication skills may not be linked to a cognitive need. However, support is still necessary to give these children equal access to educational opportunities.

To support learners with SLCN, it is important for all adults to model speech correctly. Encourage talk at every opportunity throughout the school day. Alongside this, teachers plan opportunities for children to develop their listening skills and use activities involving group work. We need to plan to introduce new words and explain their meanings, whilst challenging children to use new vocabulary in their everyday language. This includes the opportunities for children to ask questions themselves in the classroom (see Chapter 6 to read more about questioning).

In supporting children with communication difficulties we need to supplement spoken language with visuals whenever possible and think carefully about the classroom environment. We might ask ourselves: how supportive are the visual cues for learners with SLCN? Do they provide additional reinforcement of key ideas? Is text clearly presented and uncluttered? By using visual cues we support processing, comprehension and memory. Whole class approaches such as using a visual timetable and the labelling of classroom resources with signs and symbols support all children, including those with SLCN, to independently access the classroom environment.

Effective teacher planning should include the wording of clear instructions and explanations. Plans should include how questions are phrased and how adequate time will be provided for children to process the information and allow them to respond. This may include opportunities for talk, jottings and other thinking space provision. Many teachers use Makaton™ or other informal gestures to communicate non-verbally. These are augmentative communication approaches to be used alongside the verbal to make meaning clear to all children. Additional resources, such as audio recording tools, can be utilised to support children with recording their responses, or to enable an adult's instruction to be recorded and repeated. There are also many apps, talking story books and interactive websites which can be used to model language pronunciation and construction.

Socialisation

Schools are very social places, and at first glance it may appear that all children are engaging well within their peer groups. However, some children find it difficult to form social interactions with others, which may lead to social isolation, particularly for children with particular needs. As teachers we need to be sensitive to children who may lack confidence and are reluctant to engage socially, or who may not understand the 'unwritten rules' of social interaction, such as turn-taking, respecting an individual's personal space or adapting their language to the situation. There are some children with identified needs, such as Autism or Attention-Deficit Hyperactivity Disorder (ADHD), who display these traits, but these characteristics may also exhibit themselves where there is no identified need. We need to take account of children's socialisation needs and ensure that individual and collaborative opportunities are deliberately planned for.

To support learners with socialisation it is important to understand the young person's needs. It is important for teachers to gain the child's perspective to remind ourselves of what they may be experiencing. It is important to recognise how something that we may feel is insignificant could cause much stress or anxiety for a young person with socialisation difficulties. In the classroom stress and anxiety can be reduced by providing individual alternatives, choice of activity and additional scaffolding for the social elements of the tasks. For example, children can be given specific roles within group work to alleviate the uncertainty of negotiation in a social environment.

Having a well-planned and well-delivered programme of Personal, Social, Health and Economic (PSHE) in school is a good place to start to support individuals with socialisation needs. This will provide opportunities to support all learners, but particularly those with difficulties in socialising, to learn how to interact using circle time, storytelling, role play and games. Social conventions can be modelled by adults, demonstrating the skills in listening and responding, which can be practised in a 'safe' environment. The planning of PSHE lessons can be tailored to incorporate some of the needs of an individual to allow classmates to develop their understanding of these needs and how to respond in an inclusive way. It may be worthwhile to set up a buddy system where volunteers from the class support the individual, acting as role models to develop confidence or to give reminders about the appropriateness of behaviour. Use of these approaches benefits all children, including those with socialisation needs.

Self-esteem

One of the biggest barriers to learning for all children can be their own self-belief. This is particularly the case for children for whom their communication, socialisation and other needs may mean they have experienced challenges which can impact on their self-esteem. Children who are afraid to make mistakes often find it difficult to progress. For children, the security of knowing that they have many qualities and that they have the resilience to overcome setbacks is integral to being able to maximise potential. There are a number of simple things we can do as a teacher to address this, such as goal-setting, clear feedback and praise.

Giving children the opportunity to monitor their own learning and set their own goals is a way of supporting their independence and self-esteem. Assessment for learning (see Chapter 5) in lessons serves a number of purposes. One of these is to inform the children of their next steps. Making these activities independent gives the child a sense of ownership over their own learning. In order for this to be effective, clear steps to success or success criteria will be needed, to ensure that these are planned for effectively. To support this, as teachers we need to be clear with our feedback. This lets the children know exactly what is expected of them and what areas they need to focus on and so needs to be personalised for the individual child. Written feedback, whilst sometimes laborious, can have an impact. However, finding time for oral feedback is most powerful and enables teachers to be responsive to children's needs 'in the moment', providing the opportunity for enhanced participation from the child through two-way dialogue instead of one way feedback.

Praise and celebration are important for building children's self-esteem. Praising children as often as possible is essential. What they can do is far more important than what they cannot and children need to hear that they are good at things – we cannot assume that they already know that we think they are good at something. Each teacher develops their own actions of celebration with their class which can range from a simple 'high five' to a 'silent cheer'. In the example from practice 8.2, Billy's teacher used his own way of getting all of the children to praise an individual child's achievements.

Example from practice 8.2: Billy and the firefighter

Billy worked hard to achieve his goal to understand place value in his maths lesson, and he finally began to recognise tenths and hundredths more quickly and accurately. In response to a series of questions posed by his teacher, Billy put correct answers on his individual whiteboard and held them up for the teacher to see. The teacher noticed and spontaneously made the action of a firefighter directing a hose all over Billy. The teacher shouted "Billy is on fire", and the other children joined in pretending to be hosing Billy down. Billy smiled broadly as he looked around the classroom. He felt great!

Another way to raise children's self-esteem is to display their work in the school environment. It is important that children see that their hard work is valued. There is rarely space to display all children's work, so we need to ensure that, over a period of time, we rotate which children's work we choose to display. This will ensure that all the children get to see their work on display over a period of time. Some classrooms have displays curated by children where children can select their best work for themselves and take responsibility for deciding what represents their biggest achievements.

Essentially, our approach to developing children's self-esteem is to get to know them as individuals. Children will know if teachers have a genuine interest and knowing that they care will make them feel good about themselves. As teachers, we need to be positive and smile in the morning, ask questions about their weekend and reference activities that they are interested in. If children have school dinners, sitting with them to eat can be a good opportunity for conversations of this type. Children realise that this is a choice and appreciate it. It also gives us an opportunity to find out a little more about them away from the classroom environment. Building these positive relationships and in turn the mutual respect that goes with them means that getting attention in the classroom will be easier, and if we do have to use any sanctions, we are not rejecting anyone as an individual.

Maintaining attention

When planning for the needs of all children, maintaining the interest and attention of a class is among the biggest challenges a teacher can face. Lesson planning, pace, structure, preparation, the learning environment, teacher delivery and active learning all have important roles to play. For some children with additional needs maintaining attention can be a particular challenge. The best way for teachers to support these and all children to maintain attention is to be well-prepared and plan carefully, taking account of how engagement will be fostered. When planning a lesson, we need to consider the different types of tasks and activities being implemented and how long will be spent on these. The pace of a lesson is really important, and our planning needs to be flexible as we may have to deviate from a plan if things are taking too long. Sometimes this also requires breaking tasks down into smaller tasks and reducing teacher talk which children may be able to listen to only in short bursts. We need to ensure that the classroom environment is conducive to maintaining attention including seating children where they can see the teacher, with children whom they feel comfortable with and in a way that enables partner talk and group discussion. Desks need to be uncluttered, children need access to all necessary resources and distractions need to be minimised.

Teachers need to be the most interesting thing in the room when they are addressing the class. Children need to be interested in us as a person so it is important that we work hard to form positive relationships and let our personality show (we should not be afraid to use humour in our teaching). If the teacher delivering the lesson is expressive, positive and enthusiastic there is a much greater chance that the children will be too. Varying tone of voice and moving out of the 'teacher's space' is important so that we move around the classroom (Wright 2005). We must ensure that each child is an active participant in the lesson which includes all answering questions and discussing their ideas so that everyone *feels* included and that they are a valued contributor.

Conclusion

Whilst there are very many special educational needs and disabilities, these often involve needs in similar areas. In this chapter we have explored four such areas: communication, socialisation, attention and self-esteem. When there is a child in our class or setting with a specific SEND label, we can sometimes feel disempowered as teachers and feel that we do not know how to teach a child with that specific label. Switching our mindset to focus upon common aspects of best practice can be more empowering and more inclusive. As teachers we can recognise the benefits for all children when we plan for supporting children to communicate, socialise, maintain attention and have strong self-esteem. Ultimately, we need to plan for and teach the child and not the SEND label.

Points to ponder

What is good practice to support children with an identified need? How does this support all children?

How can adults be deployed to ensure that children with the most complex needs are most effectively supported yet independent and autonomous learners?

How can differentiation strategies be made most inclusive, whilst still supporting children with additional needs?

References

The Communication Trust. (2014) *Let's Talk About It*. Available at: www.thecommunicationtrust. org.uk/

Department for Education and Department for Health. (2015) Special educational needs and disability code of practice: 0 to 25 years. Available at: www.gov.uk/government/publications/ send-code-of-practice-0-to-25

Education, Audiovisual and Culture Executive Agency. (2010). *Organisation of the education system in Liechtenstein*. Available at: https://estudandoeducacao.files.wordpress.com/2011/05/liechtenstein.pdf

Lebeer, J., Birta-Szekely, N., Demeter, K., Bohács, K., Candeias, A.A., Sønnesyn, G., Partanen, P., Dawson, L. (2011) *Re-assessing the current assessment practice of children with special education needs, school psychology international*. Full report available at: www.daffodilproject.org

OECD. (2007) *Students with disabilities, learning difficulties and disadvantages: Statistics and indicators*. Paris: OECD/CERI.

Vickerman, P. (2007) Training physical education teachers to include children with special educational needs: Perspectives from physical education initial teacher training providers. *European Physical Education Review*, 13(3), 385–402.

Wright, D. (2005) *There's no need to shout!: The primary teacher's guide to successful behaviour management*. Cheltenham: Nelson Thornes.

9

Outdoor learning

Sarah Hindmarsh and Susan Hunt

If we recognise that learning takes place everywhere and is not limited to the formal environment of the classroom we might ask the question, why not learn outdoors? This chapter explores what is distinctive about learning outdoors and why teachers should plan for rich experiences in the outdoor environment, whether that be a corner of the playground, the grassy field, a patch of woodland, seashore or field studies centre. We explore how to plan for learning outdoors, considering approaches that are effective when working with children of 3–11 years and use illustrative examples to shed light on effective and easily accessed approaches. For learning outdoors to be successful, teachers need to be well prepared, confident and resourceful. This chapter explores the 'why' and 'how' of planning for outdoor learning that can have real benefits for children.

Why outdoors?

Outdoor learning experiences offer rich rewards to the child. Children experience cognitive (acquisition of knowledge), emotional (development of attitudes), social (building relationships) and physical (developing skills) benefits from outdoor experiences (Dillon et al. 2005). Research shows that outdoor learning offers a richly immersive experience where the child can connect to the environment through learning which is multi-sensory. Such learning is memorable for its ability to really engage the learner and make connections for them across many subject boundaries. For example, the child exploring the woodland with their class as they search for invertebrates hidden under logs and in the leaf litter will be learning and developing their scientific skills of observation, identification and classification whist at the same time developing social skills of turn-taking and conversation. Children might respond artistically to what they are seeing, they could build shelters for the animals that live in the habitat and develop physically as they move, climb and balance. Alternatively, using the woodland as a stimulus, the class might engage with storytelling or creative writing. Teachers can exploit the rich outdoor environment to plan for such cross-curricular and multi-sensory learning opportunities, which encourage children to cooperate with one another and develop a wide range of skills. These opportunities offer the child first-hand experiences of the natural world that charities such as the UK-based RSPB and the National Trust call for as an essential part of a healthy childhood (Moss 2012; RSPB 2010). With some children having limited exposure to the outdoors and many children (and adults) living increasingly sedentary lives, opportunities to engage in out of classroom experiences as part of schooling are essential (Tremblay et al. 2010). As teachers, we aspire for all children to grow up as healthy adults with a lifelong attitude of care for the environment to support them to be responsible citizens and future custodians of our precious planet's resource.

In order for children to take risks in their learning, they need to feel safe and secure to do so. Nora, Sofie and Anders, in their example from practice 9.1, demonstrate the importance of trust in encouraging children to take risks. When children explore together they talk together, play, cooperate and problem-solve. Interactions with teachers are often more informal when learning takes place outdoors, and the boundaries, real or imagined, between teacher and child are lessened. The outdoors offers a rich environment for the learner to experience success through its ability to excite and challenge. Children develop this self-efficacy through outdoor learning, developing their belief in their own capabilities to succeed (Carrier 2009).

Example from practice 9.1: Supporting physical risk taking

Nora, Sofie and Anders, Kindergarten student teachers in Northern Norway, set up an area of woodland for physical risk taking for a group of 3–5-year-old children. They chose a patch of steeply sided natural woodland and suspended rope structures among the trees. Nora, Sofie and Anders each encouraged the children to climb on the rope structures. The children were free to run and climb, supervised carefully but not over protectively by the student teachers. Secure among trusted adults, the children demonstrated playful curiosity, pushing themselves just as far as they felt comfortable to do.

Residential field work with children offers an immersive experience in which children and adults alike can gain from time away from the usual classroom environment. It may not be possible to travel very far but a residential field work opportunity can offer many benefits including for professional development and team building as described in the example from practice of student teachers participating in residential experiences (example from practice 9.2).

Example from practice 9.2: Student teachers engaging in field work

Student teachers at the beginning of their university undergraduate course participate in a short residential fieldwork experience where they learn to explore all the possibilities for learning in a historic village environment in England. Some students are a little reluctant at first to don wellies and waterproofs, climb hills, wade in streams and swing from tree branches. However, by the end of three days, they find that they can more confidently apply their sketching skills, use and interpret historical source material and design a risk assessment for working with pupils outdoors. As the students walked over the moors, got muddy, read maps and sheltered from the rain, they found that friendships were forged and confidence gained. In this way they began to develop the self-efficacy which, as teachers, will prepare them for the rich opportunities that taking children outdoors allows.

Student teachers in their university undergraduate course undertake a residential field work visit to a small island in Norway. They experience science at the seashore, creative writing, cooking in the outdoors, drama, history and wooden tool making. This rich experience allowed the students to acquire the skills they would need as teachers and to plan for cross-curricular learning, developing confidence as they worked with their peers.

Breaking down barriers

Teachers can face many barriers to taking learning outdoors which, if not addressed, might result in missed opportunities for learning. In a crowded curriculum it can be difficult to make time for outdoor learning and yet, if opportunities are taken to plan for cross-curricular learning, much can be gained from experiences which are engaging and memorable. Outdoor learning should be embedded in the ethos of the school and, ideally, a regular feature in the school timetable. These outdoor experiences are possible in all schools, regardless of facilities and location. It is important to realise that learning outdoors can be making use of the playground or the flowerpots as well as field work in a distant location. Whatever the location, outdoor learning requires good prior preparation (purposeful planning) so that we, as teachers, feel confident and know what to expect to prepare for quality learning and effective management of risks.

Teachers need a degree of confidence and experience to plan for learning outside the classroom. Good preparation includes spending time in the specific outdoor environment, considering the possibilities for learning and individual needs. Careful attention is needed in planning for how children will be introduced to an unfamiliar area and encouraged to access the learning opportunities. Children need to be carefully briefed, in an age-appropriate way, so that they understand their responsibilities and teacher expectations. For teachers less experienced in outdoor learning, the support of more experienced colleagues can be valuable. The next section considers what successful planning in the outdoor environment looks like and offers some suggestions for successful approaches.

Some key concerns for teachers are summarised in Table 9.1.

TABLE 9.1 Commons concerns about learning outdoors

Teacher considerations	Possible steps to take
Health and safety risks	Follow school policy and format for risk assessment. Visit the location to become familiar with possible hazards, assessing the level of risk and put into place appropriate controls.
	Share with additional adults and children as appropriate.
	Ensure children and adults are suitably dressed so that the activity can take place, whatever the weather.

(Continued)

Teacher considerations	Possible steps to take
Expectations for learning	Plan learning intentions and success criteria in a similar way to indoor learning but be prepared for incidental learning. Follow up children's interests and support children in asking and answering their questions.
Behaviour management	Make sure expectations for behaviour are clear.
	Explain boundaries (these can be marked where appropriate, for example, coloured string around trees or cones).
	Different rules may apply, regarding how children move around the location or how they look after the environment, and these need to clear and potentially modelled or practised.
Teacher role	This will include planning, risk assessment and maintaining a safe environment. The teacher needs to be prepared to model active learning, specific skills and enthusiasm. The teacher anticipates and encourages children's questions and exploration as well as observing and assessing learning.
The role of other adults	Share planning, expectations (for both learning and behaviour) and risk assessments with all adults.
	Explain how they can best support the children, perhaps planning for each adult to work with a carefully selected small group. Support adults with specialist knowledge, for example, by providing tree identification guides and a local map.
	Ensure adults are provided with a timetable for the outdoor learning experience.
Getting to know your local area	To support continuity and progression in learning and experiences, a whole-school overview is helpful. As a staff, look at the opportunities afforded by the school grounds, places within walking distance and those you could reach by public transport or other means (an audit tool could be used to support this). Involve children's families and governors as they might have relevant expertise or help gain access to local places, such as allotments.
Parental concerns	To alleviate parental concerns, share information about the benefits of learning outdoors. This could be through a newsletter, blog or parents' meeting. Display artwork, items collected, photographs of children taking part in activities and learning outdoors, with a clear explanation of the learning that took place. Invite parents to participate in activities where appropriate.
Rain, wind and other weather	Ensure there is space to store appropriate clothing – wellies, waterproofs, gloves, hats, etc. – in each classroom. Small plastic greenhouses are ideal for storing wellies outside. Encourage parents to contribute spare clothing so that all children can keep warm and have a change of clothes if they get muddy or wet. However, high winds should be avoided. In the summer, make sure all children have sun-hats and have applied sun-screen. Different weather conditions can be seen as a prompt for a variety of first-hand learning experiences, particularly 'seasonal change' and exploring types of weather. Staff should model positive attitudes to different weather conditions and pre-empt negative comments. For example, a brisk march on a cold day or encouraging children to walk in the shade on a hot day.

Teacher considerations	Possible steps to take
Accessibility	Consider the needs of all children in the class when planning outdoor activities and writing risk assessments. Plan strategies to support children who might be challenged by any change to routine, the terrain, open spaces and outdoor noises. Some children benefit from an individual explanation beforehand of why they are going outside, what they will be doing and what to expect, perhaps using a visual timetable or photographs.
	Ensure additional adults are well briefed and/or aware of the needs of the children. They can also be involved in planning for individual children.
Anxiety	Some children may be anxious about going outside. Risk assessments can be shared with children in an age-appropriate way, and they can be involved in writing them. Give reassurance and praise achievements to develop confidence and self-esteem. Share their successes with parents, the class and others (as appropriate). Give children a responsibility, such as photographer, carrying or handing out resources.
	Provide spare outdoor clothing.

Planning for cross-curricular opportunities

The multi-sensory nature and 'real-life' experiences offered by the outdoor environment make it suitable for planning across the curriculum, where concepts that are abstract can be brought to life. Use of the immediate locality of the school will make learning meaningful to children, enable them to share their own knowledge and ideas and give them the opportunity to share learning outside of school with family members. A starting point for planning could be at a whole staff or age phase meeting, discussing the affordances for learning in the school grounds and immediate vicinity of the school. The example from Emily's practice shows how she worked with colleagues to plan outdoor learning in the local area of the school (example from practice 9.3). Experiences can be mapped across the curriculum and throughout the school, securing progression in knowledge and skills development.

Example from practice 9.3: Emily plans a 'houses' trail

For a topic on 'houses and homes', Emily and her colleagues planned a walking trail around the town for the 5–7 years olds in their classes. The children looked closely at the variety of styles of houses, built at different times and for different purposes. Emily had prepared laminated photographs of the houses for the children to 'spot', and then at each location the adults engaged children in using observational and reasoning skills. Having researched about the location in advance, the adults helped the children to ask questions and discover their locality in a whole new way, leading to learning in history, geography, science and mathematics. This experience was then followed up in school, across the curriculum, including using programmable toys to 'visit' houses on a grid.

Planning for unexpected learning opportunities

Different types of outdoor learning require different levels of planning. Plans for outdoor learning could take the form of teacher-led lessons that have sharply focused learning objectives, clear success criteria and tightly planned activities and assessment. Alternatively, planning for outdoor learning could incorporate experiences that are more open-ended, such as giving children cameras, paint boxes or sketchbooks to capture seasonal images such as spring flowers. Whatever the level of planning, we need to identify the learning that we want to take place but recognise that the outdoor context can often promote unplanned opportunities for learning. This is a key advantage and any spontaneous learning can be followed up in the classroom or in a future session outside. For this reason, teachers sometimes use the term 'learning intention' rather than 'learning objective'. Our subsequent reflections during and after an experience should take account of any unplanned learning outcomes. The example from Tom's practice demonstrates the benefit of planning for and building upon children's interests in the outdoor environment (example from practice 9.4).

Example from practice 9.4: Tom and the walk in the woods in Autumn

In Tom's school, classes of 5–7 years olds regularly walked to the local woods to carry out activities linked to seasonal change. In Autumn, the learning intention for the walk was for children to use their senses to describe the sounds, smells and sights they believed were special to Autumn. Tom briefed all adults, including parent helpers, to support with this: questioning and encouraging where appropriate. When the children returned to class in the afternoon, they drew on this sensory experience to generate descriptive vocabulary and phrases. The children shared, discussed and subsequently used their phrases in poetry writing. On the walk and in the classroom afterwards, the children were fascinated by leaf 'skeletons' which led to discussion of plant life cycles and the application of scientific inquiry skills through the use of magnifying glasses and microscopes. This valuable learning arose from the children's interests on the walk and Tom's ability to build upon these interests.

It is important to recognise that our planning for outdoors might be either pro-active or responsive to children's interests and ideas. Due to the open-ended nature of the outdoor environment, we need to be prepared for children to be curious and ask questions that might lead to further learning outcomes or possibilities for us to follow now or in the future. In Tom's example, an important factor was the amount of time available for children to explore the woodland. This led to deeper levels of engagement because children could follow, and become immersed in, their own interest.

As with lessons that take place indoors, the learning intention and success criteria is often shared before the children leave the classroom, then revisited during or after the outdoor experience. Further assessment opportunities can be provided as children complete tasks, perhaps solving a problem, making observational sketches, answering questions or recording data in a tally chart. This information can then form the basis of further lessons indoors. As the outdoor context provides a rich opportunity to develop social, emotional and physical aspects of learning, we might plan for and share learning intentions in these aspects also.

Regular time for child-led exploration of the outdoors is a key feature of the Forest School approach to learning. This approach has other distinctive features, such as the opportunity for children to take supported risks and the development of trust (Knight 2013), that set it apart from other forms of outdoor learning. The benefits of this approach are also arguably beyond those of more traditional outdoor 'lessons', in particular the impact on the 'whole' child. For example, self-esteem, confidence, independence, social skills, decision-making skills and environmental awareness are enhanced using this approach (Constable 2014). Chloe's explanation of how the Forest School approach enhanced her practice is included in her example from practice 9.5.

Example from practice 9.5: Chloe and 'Superworm'

As part of Chloe's initial teacher education course, she completed Level 1 and 2 Forest School training. She was keen to apply her learning on her next placement and chose to use a picture book *Superworm* by Julia Donaldson (2014). Chloe explained:

'After completing my Level 1 and 2 Forest School training, I was eager to use the outdoor environment across the curriculum in order to make learning meaningful and memorable for my 5–6 year old children. In addition to the holistic benefits of the outdoors, providing children with the freedom to direct their own learning enabled me to channel children's interests and learn alongside them. For example, a group of children displayed a keen interest in insects and other wildlife, beginning to question habitats and food chains. This provided a perfect opportunity to tailor learning to the children's interests in order to develop science enquiry skills.

I used the children's curiosities to guide our learning by creating science story sacks that encouraged child-led investigations. After reading the *Superworm* story, the children raised their own scientific enquiry questions. For example, where do Superworm's friends live? The children then self-selected equipment to pack in their sacks that they felt would help them to solve their enquiry. This enabled children to think through the procedural nature of their investigations and justify their choices before taking their sacks outdoors to explore. Completely immersed in their learning environment, these children developed their abilities to investigate, record and use their developing scientific vocabulary'.

Outdoor learning, like all learning, requires careful assessment throughout (see Chapter 5). Assessment of outdoor learning can be supported by making assessment notes 'in the field', including of children's level of interest, curiosity and their comments. This will provide strong evidence of their attitude and engagement, as well as their interests, understanding and misconceptions. Recording the questions that children ask can be used to plan opportunities for further exploration, if not possible at the time, or opportunities to guide them in finding answers.

Conclusion

The benefits gained from learning outdoors give a clear rationale for the time and effort that goes into the planning and preparation. Much effort goes into resourcing outdoor activities but this can be shared with colleagues and is ultimately worthwhile. Sharing knowledge of suitable sites and activities for learning is a good way of finding new and different ways of using outdoor learning. Barriers can be overcome and should not be a deterrent, for example, a local bus can be used if the journey is too far to walk. Finally, we need to be prepared to be flexible; learning may take a different direction from the initial intention, but this approach will be beneficial for both children and teachers.

Points to ponder

What might the concerns of parents be with outdoor learning and how could you reassure them?

What might a child find challenging or worrisome in the outdoors and how could you gently encourage and adapt your planning to support them? What could you do, in your preparation, which would make them feel safe and secure so that they could take risks?

How will your planning enable you to recognise and take account of the 'unplanned learning' that occurs in the outdoors?

References

Carrier, S. (2009) The effects of outdoor science lessons with elementary school students on preservice teachers' self-efficacy'. *Journal of Elementary Science Education*, 21(2), 35–48.

Constable, K. (2014) *Bringing the forest school approach to your early years practice*. Abingdon: Routledge.

Dillon, J., Morris, M., O'Donnell, L., Reid, A, Rickinson, M. & Scott, W. (2005) *Engaging and learning with the outdoors: The final report of the outdoor classroom in a rural context action research project*. Berkshire: National Foundation for Educational Research [NFER].

Donaldson, J. (2014) *Superworm*. London: Scholastic.

Knight, S. (2013) *Forest school and outdoor learning in the early years*. London: Sage.

Moss, S. (2012) *Natural childhood*. Swindon: The National Trust.

The Royal Society for the Protection of Birds [RSPB] (2010) *Every child outdoors* [online]. Available at: www.rspb.org.uk/Images/everychildoutdoors_tcm9-259689.pdf

Tremblay, M. S., Colley, R. C., Saunders, T. J., Healey, G. N. & Owen, N. (2010) Physiological and health implications of a sedentary lifestyle. *Applied Physiology, Nutrition, and Metabolism*, 35(6), 725–740.

10

Planning for sustainability

Elaine Haywood

Introduction

This chapter looks at the concept of sustainability and the contribution this can make to the primary curriculum and classroom. Planning for sustainable development education in primary schools could seem challenging, as potential topics are complex and there is often no specific curriculum guidance to form a clear framework. Aspects of sustainability could be considered in many subject areas: in geography, working on climate zones; in science, looking at materials and the water cycle; and in English, looking at literature concerned with climate change and human migration. Topics have a tendency to be thought provoking and often cross-curricular in nature. Arguably however, a broad and balanced education has a responsibility to ensure children have relevant knowledge and experience to inform their own sustainable choices in the present and the future.

In this chapter the rationale for including sustainability in the primary curriculum is expressed, and the following sections explore possibilities for including rights education, the protection of the natural world and global citizenship.

Why include education for sustainable development?

The motivation to include education for sustainability in the curriculum comes from a realisation that the problems created by humanity need a global response. Action needs to be taken across countries as resources diminish, and conflict causes destruction in many parts of the world. The impact of human activity on the natural environment has implications for this generation and future generations. In order to make a difference, children need to be informed and willing to influence change.

Part of the solution can be seen as making our lives more sustainable. The most commonly quoted definition of sustainable development was made in the Brundtland Report (1987): 'Sustainable development is development that meets the needs of the present without compromising the ability of future generations to meet their own needs'. This principle includes sustainable relationships within human society and the natural world. Subsequent global summits between nations have developed the aims further, culminating in the United Nations Sustainable Development Goals agreed in 2015 and looking towards achievement in 2030. These goals include specific aims for education:

> By 2030, ensure that all learners acquire the knowledge and skills needed to promote sustainable development, including, among others, through education for sustainable development and sustainable lifestyles, human rights, gender equality, promotion of a culture of peace and non-violence, global citizenship and appreciation of cultural diversity and of culture's contribution to sustainable development.
>
> (United Nations, 2015:17)

The Earth Charter (2010) sums this up succinctly as 'bringing forth a global society founded on respect for nature, universal human rights, economic justice and a culture of peace'. Under section IV Democracy, Nonviolence and Peace, the charter specifically outlines the role of education in 'providing all, especially children and youth with educational opportunities that empower them to contribute actively to sustainable development'. This is a key concept. Children can not only learn about the world but can be encouraged to consider critically the issues involved and find ways to act on that knowledge.

Non-government organisations, such as Oxfam, are actively involved in working for more sustainable futures for citizens across the world, and education is seen to be key in achieving this aim. Oxfam UK (2015) identifies the role of a global citizen, who not only has knowledge about the wider world but is inspired to be involved in making the world more sustainable and equitable. To this end, they produce a wide range of materials to support planning in schools. However, teachers have to be aware that there are multiple points of view and planning should enable critical thinking and awareness, in order that children can begin to make decisions for themselves.

What does sustainability look like in the primary school and classroom?

The Global Goals encompass a wide range of concerns and there will need to be decisions about how to present these issues to children as they progress through school. Areas that could be considered include: Rights and Relationships, Protection of the Natural World and what it might mean to be a Global Citizen. The following sections look at these in turn with some examples from practice.

Rights and relationships

The Global Goals include a clear emphasis on the importance of human relationships in order to achieve a fairer and peaceful world. This includes looking at gender, diversity and conflict resolution. Children's experience of community in school can be seen as a microcosm of the wider social environment and a place to begin to understand what it means to be part of a wider diverse society. Relationships are an important part of the experience of school and can encourage children to have positive and accepting attitudes.

Elements of this aspect of sustainability have always been an important part of primary education. As a child begins in nursery, they need to adapt to the challenge of making relationships with children and adults that are not part of their immediate family. This is supported by teachers giving clear guidelines and a safe accepting environment. Children are given choice and encouraged to work together.

Older children are socialised into the community of school, with explicit expectations for acceptable behaviour, through school and classroom rules and procedures. This is an important part of planning for your own classroom. Article 12 of the Rights of the Child states that children have the right to be heard and this is taken seriously in schools, where school councils give children a voice in policy and often in the recruitment of staff. In your classroom you can encourage children to construct rules for acceptable behaviour and to find ways to resolve difficulties, be inclusive and treat adults and children with respect. This is covered in more detail in Chapter 3, looking at ways to promote an environment for inclusion, but can also be viewed as an aspect of sustainability.

Some schools have taken this idea further and have taken part in the United Nations Children's Fund Rights Respecting Schools Programme. The programme has four key areas: well-being, participation, relationships and self-esteem. The website provides training and lesson planning ideas. Obviously, the programme is designed to be a whole school commitment – but the free resources could provide inspiration for your classroom and practice.

One school that has followed this programme has been impressed by the difference it has made for their children, both in school and when they leave to move on to secondary education, as the following example from practice 10.1 shows:

Example from practice 10.1: Rights Respecting School Award at City Primary School

Yasmin Khalique, Jerome Lantelme, Sarah Smith, Heather Ryan work as the Unicef's Rights Respecting School Award (RRSA) team at City Primary School. They explain how their work is an integral part of their school's culture and values.

We are a school that goes to great lengths to listen to our children, where they have a voice and are encouraged to express their thoughts and where our differences, as well as similarities, are respected and celebrated. We actively encourage both children and adults alike to become compassionate and caring towards each other and our environment. The programmes of RRSA work continually reinforce an awareness of children's rights and encourage positive and inclusive language and behaviour. We seek to extend that understanding beyond our school and into families and local communities through dialogue, arts projects and media. A quote from a recently retired Head Teacher of five years illustrates the long-lasting positive impact that coming to our school has on pupils.

Earlier this year I met with one of the Assistant Head Teachers at our feeder Secondary School. She told me that that our children really stand out. They are the ones who show a real thirst for learning, who are mature, sensible and independent. They are the students who all the teachers want in their tutor groups. She told me we should feel very proud of the work we do at our school.

Yasmin Khalique, Jerome Lantelme, Sarah Smith, Heather Ryan: RRSA Team.

Protection of the natural world

The primary school curriculum has always included an appreciation of the natural world, and this develops across the curriculum particularly in science, from looking at the signs of spring with young children to understanding the complex web of adaptations shown in a given habitat. There is a strong argument that suggests children, increasingly based in urban communities, will only value the environment if they have direct experiences and interaction with the natural world. The Forest School movement (see the forestschoolassociation.org) can be seen as part of this initiative to give children a chance to learn in the outdoors and to experience first-hand the issues in their local environment (see Chapter 9). Other opportunities are present in the school grounds, where gardening clubs can give children the chance to see how plants develop and how food is grown. Some schools may go further and look after a variety of animals onsite. Richard Dunne, Head Teacher at a school in Surrey, bases his whole curriculum around big questions, which include 'where does our food come from?' The answer, in this case, is often it comes from the school grounds and straight into the school kitchen. Children are encouraged to look at local supplies and the difference in buying organic and more industrially produced food. This education can encourage children to investigate choices and the issues surrounding production.

In addition, outdoor learning can provide a catalyst for change. Children can learn about the environment, but also learn to be active in protecting their locality as this case study, from a lesson planned by a recently qualified teacher demonstrates in example from practice 10.2:

Example from practice 10.2: Marc's outdoor lesson

'On a crisp autumn morning, a class of children aged 4–5, put their boots on and followed their teacher outdoors. "Today we are learning how to describe autumn". The children were expected to talk about the sights and sounds of autumn to inspire their poetry writing that week. The poems never got written though. It wasn't that the activity hadn't inspired them, the learning just took a very different journey.

Letting go of the weekly plan was the first step for teaching children about sustainability. Whilst walking, children noticed a litter problem on their 'special lane' to school. By the time they had made it back to school, the attention had shifted from autumn scenes to a frantic debate about litter and fly tipping.

For the rest of the week, the children were guided in how to negotiate plans to address this issue in their local area. They developed a strong attachment to their place in the world, wanting to make a difference to their local area. The writing that week became campaign poster making, the debate continued with podcasts published to the class blog for parents to listen to and further visits were made out-side in an attempt to clean up the litter. Building on young children's interest was key to the success of teaching sustainability'.

Marc Faulder

Children are often aware of the need to recycle, and local waste collection sites can be a local source of seeing how this works in practice. Visits can be arranged to these sites, and children can learn about how many household goods can go on to become a resource that is used again. However, even a very effective recycling scheme cannot dispose of every unwanted item. Children can also investigate what happens to materials that have no future use. One student teacher found children in her class had no idea what happened to this type of waste and a lesson developed to raise their understanding in example from practice 10.3:

Example from practice 10.3: Megan supports learning about landfill sites

Every day in Megan's class, the children watched *Newsround* in the morning. One of the topics, which came up often, was about plastic in the ocean and rubbish dis-posal, and the children were very curious about this, often asking questions about where rubbish went once we put it in the bin. Megan decided to take advantage of the children's curiosity and plan a couple of lessons about where rubbish goes and the decomposition process. She decided that it would be beneficial for the children to see the effects of a landfill and thought that making their own landfills would be a good, hands-on experience, which would help them to see the process overtime. Megan also thought that this would be good to help them see why it is difficult to get rid of plastic and why we are trying to cut down on our plastic usage. The children made their own landfill sites in plastic bottles layering a mixture of card, paper, wool and plastic under topsoil and water. The bottles were left for three weeks, and the de-composition rates of the materials compared. Megan felt this made children aware of issues surrounding the environment and where their rubbish goes and heard the chil-dren discussing the fact that plastic is hard to remove from the environment. Future lessons could be planned to consider the possible solutions to using landfill sites.

Another lively take on recycling made links to the science topic of materials in example from practice 10.4:

Example from practice 10.4: Learning about the potential of recycling

We had been completing a unit on materials, and I wanted to draw in recycling after a child had chosen to read a book the week prior called *Michael Recycle*. The children loved this book, and we had a big discussion about what recycling was and why we do it. Surprisingly, a lot of the class didn't really understand why we recycle or what it really was despite using recycling paper each day in school. The homework for that week was to bring in used toilet rolls and other materials we could use again.

The lesson began with different materials on each desk that I had collected. As an introduction, I told the class that this afternoon we are a recycling centre and we need to sort all our materials into different sections (paper and card, plastic, glass, metal). As a team they decided where each material went and took them to the appropriate box at the front of the class.

From this I gave some general input about recycling and different things that could happen if we recycle more. From this I told the children we would be focusing on 'Reuse' and that we had a special visitor coming in to give us a task.

Teacher in role – I dressed as Michael Recycle, a superhero, which consisted of a green top MR on my chest, an eye mask and bin bag cape. The children loved this and were really engaged. The task was set, 'Can we reuse the toilet rolls you have been collecting for another purpose? Begin to think of ideas and create something with another purpose'. Children could use all the materials that had been collected over the week along with paint and glue and other craft stuff available.

'Michael Recycle' came back at the end of the session to check what they had made which gave a motivation to get it done. The children loved this and came up with better ideas than I could to reuse their toilet rolls: I remember a pencil pot, a penguin and a car.

The children continued this at home and for the next couple of weeks continued to bring in things they had recycled to show and tell.

The impact of the lesson had changed the way children were considering materials beyond the claims of the science curriculum and the expected learning objectives.

The problems facing the world are not simple cases of one side right and another side wrong. Environmental education can involve more than nature study. Children can begin to engage with the competing claims on our environment and how choices have to be made in order to manage these sustainably. Often opportunities exist very close to the school location, and even as part of the school grounds, which can engage the children in looking at ways to maintain, protect and develop their own environment. Learning through Landscapes is an organisation that could provide starting points for developing outdoor learning and an appreciation for the world on our own doorsteps.

Global citizenship

John Donne's assertion that no man is an island was never more appropriate than it is today. Each country is reliant on the global economy, and our lives are interlinked with peoples across the globe. One easy way to demonstrate this is to look at what children have eaten for a meal during the day and identify the many different countries that have been involved in supplying the produce. Often children will be encouraged to consider the difficulties faced by communities in the Third World, and this feels acceptable as one starting point, but this can lead to a stereotypical view of places and people, without the awareness of the history and continuing exploitation that has taken place. Children can look at how trade has been balanced in favour of countries who can market and process raw materials, rather than the producers of the raw materials. It becomes less about charity and more about making the world a fairer place. Oxfam UK (2015) has presented its view of a global citizen as one who not only has knowledge about the wider world but is inspired to be involved in making the world more sustainable and equitable. This view is also encapsulated in definitions around global competence and really reinforces the crucial need to consider sustainability in our planning:

> Global competence is the capacity to examine local, global, and intercultural issues; to understand and appreciate the perspectives and world views of others; to engage in open, appropriate, and effective interactions with people from different cultures; and to act for collective well-being and sustainable development.
>
> Asia Society 2018:8

There are many starting points for including sustainability in the curriculum we offer children. One well-resourced starting point could be the World's Largest Lesson – a growing resource that introduces the Global Goals. Practical experiences can start with the creative use of the school's grounds, looking at issues that concern the local community, as well as appreciating the challenges faced globally. Rights and responsibilities in the school community are a model for engagement in the wider world. School and community events around charitable projects can be a starting place: the soft version of global citizenship (Andreotti 2014).

Technology can provide ways to make direct links and relationships with children in schools across the globe, and there are opportunities for teachers to take part in exchange programmes. Books and stories give the opportunity to empathise with situations and people we may never meet. Our children, as educated global citizens, may come to be active in ensuring a fairer and inclusive future.

Points to ponder

Which year groups would you want to engage with specific sustainability issues?

How will you judge the success of lessons concerned with sustainability? Can you identify progress in children's learning?

What is the role of primary education in creating a more sustainable future?

References

Asia Society. (2018) *Teaching for global competencies in a rapidly changing world.* Paris: OECD Publishing.

Brundtland, G. (1987) *Report of the world commission on environment and development: Our common future.* [online] Available at: www.un-documents.net/our-common-future.pdf.

de Andreotti, V. O. (2014) Soft versus critical global citizenship education. In: McCloskey, S., ed., *Development education in policy and practice.* London: Palgrave Macmillan, 21–31.

Earth Charter International (2010) The earth charter [online]. Available at: https://earthcharter. org/read-the-earth-charter/preamble/ [reproduced as an appendix in: *Journal of Education for Sustainable Development,* 4(2), 317–324.

United Nations. (2015) *Transforming our world: The 2030 agenda for sustainable development.* New York: UN Publishing.

11

Lesson as narrative

Nicky-Jane Kerr-Gilbert and Eleanor Power

Are you sitting comfortably? Then we will begin...

The primary classroom is a place of stories and for stories (Gudmundsdottir 1991:207). For many class teachers, reading the class story is a favourite time of day; everyone enjoys a good book! Many primary teachers are natural storytellers, with the children hanging on every word to find out what happens next to Lyra, Hermione, Wilbur or Amazing Grace.

Once upon a story

Stories, metaphors, anecdotes and analogies have been used to communicate ideas and to teach others since time began (Parkin 1998:1). In stories, we organise and tie together events and information to make these meaningful (Egan 1985:399). A well-crafted story or narrative can draw the reader in and carry them along on a journey exploring new ideas and emotions: there are highs and lows; dilemmas and resolutions; and ultimately conclusions. Indeed, there may well be cliff-hangers. Given that our aim as teachers is to engage and motivate our learners (DfE 2011), to introduce them to new ideas and to challenge them with new learning, we need to similarly consider how to carry children along a journey of learning, navigating their course through the lesson.

The novelist and academic, Antonia Byatt, maintains that storytelling is 'as much part of human nature as breath and the circulation of blood' (2000:166). Indeed, we make sense of the world around us through the construction of personal narratives, according to Bruner (1986). This is equally the case with wordless picture books (for example, by authors such as Shaun Tan, Jeannie Baker and David Wiesner) where the author invites the reader to draw out their own inferences. Narratives bring a sense of structure to our lives. They help us to organise and make sense of the un- familiar or the unclear (Gudmundsdottir 1991). In schools, children are taught how to appreciate a well-written narrative and how to construct their own; so, what if the well-constructed lesson could follow a similar format?

In this chapter, student teachers reflect upon the similarities they found between reading a story to a class and planning a lesson, their voices are captured throughout.

They found their collaborative thinking around the lesson as narrative influenced the way they planned lessons and supported them in planning both creatively and effectively. In this chapter, effective use of stimuli, plot and resolution within lesson planning are explored as potential scaffolds for thinking about lessons and to ultimately help us to craft engaging, coherent and memorable learning experiences for the children we teach (summarised in Figure 11.1).

Hooking the children in

Without suggesting there is a formulaic approach to reading a story aloud, there is nevertheless some consensus about the most effective ways to read aloud to a class, providing entertainment value alongside learning and an opportunity to relax and enjoy the communal and enriching experience of listening to a story. If we begin to unpick and distil this experience, we discover some common threads that interestingly link to some prominently recognised ways of organising lesson planning.

To begin, the storyteller needs to know something about the audience; to amuse, enthuse, entertain and motivate them, 'hooking' them in from the outset and keeping them interested through the twists and turns of the story. In this way, the teacher is similar to the storyteller. As Anna (a student teacher) explained a good lesson is all about, 'making sure the children are involved, hook them, make them excited'.

Effective reading aloud adds interpretation and makes text memorable. The storyteller uses expression, punctuation, tone, volume and silent moments in voice and body language to create an atmosphere, and the effective teacher similarly varies their voice, pitch and volume; uses pause; and employs body language to draw children's attention and provide emphasis to key points. As teachers, like storytellers, we use our voice and our body language to set the mood or atmosphere in the classroom.

The beginning of a story hooks the reader in and previews what may be to come. In crafting their narrative, the author will consider the needs of their audience (the reader) and how to engage them from the onset. Consider the power of the following opening lines:

> I am drowning in this roaring silence.
>
> *Pig Heart Boy* by Malorie Blackman (2011)

> The night Max wore his wolf suit and made mischief of one kind and another his mother called him 'WILD THING!' and Max said 'I'LL EAT YOU UP!' so he was sent to bed without eating anything.
>
> *Where the Wild Things Are* by Maurice Sendak (1984)

> Everybody knows the story of the Three Little Pigs. Or at least they think they do. But I'll let you in on a little secret. Nobody knows the real story, because nobody has ever heard my side of the story. I'm the Wolf.
>
> *The True Story of the Three Little Pigs* by Jon Scieszka (1989)

> When Gregor opened his eyes he had the distinct impression that someone was watching him.
>
> *Gregor the Overlander* by Suzanne Collins (1993)

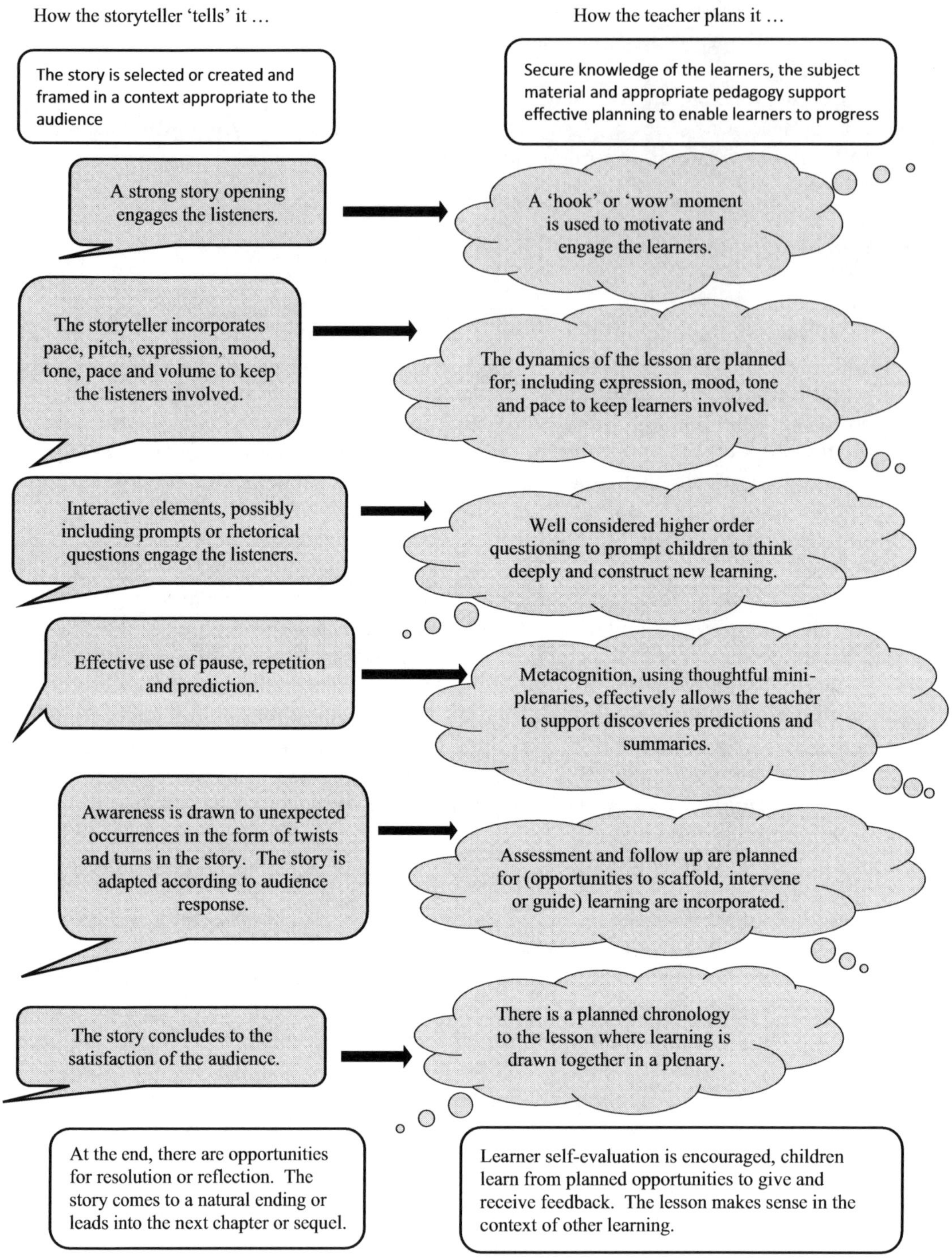

How the storyteller 'tells' it …   How the teacher plans it …

The story is selected or created and framed in a context appropriate to the audience

Secure knowledge of the learners, the subject material and appropriate pedagogy support effective planning to enable learners to progress

A strong story opening engages the listeners.

A 'hook' or 'wow' moment is used to motivate and engage the learners.

The storyteller incorporates pace, pitch, expression, mood, tone, pace and volume to keep the listeners involved.

The dynamics of the lesson are planned for; including expression, mood, tone and pace to keep learners involved.

Interactive elements, possibly including prompts or rhetorical questions engage the listeners.

Well considered higher order questioning to prompt children to think deeply and construct new learning.

Effective use of pause, repetition and prediction.

Metacognition, using thoughtful mini-plenaries, effectively allows the teacher to support discoveries predictions and summaries.

Awareness is drawn to unexpected occurrences in the form of twists and turns in the story. The story is adapted according to audience response.

Assessment and follow up are planned for (opportunities to scaffold, intervene or guide) learning are incorporated.

The story concludes to the satisfaction of the audience.

There is a planned chronology to the lesson where learning is drawn together in a plenary.

At the end, there are opportunities for resolution or reflection. The story comes to a natural ending or leads into the next chapter or sequel.

Learner self-evaluation is encouraged, children learn from planned opportunities to give and receive feedback. The lesson makes sense in the context of other learning.

FIGURE 11.1 How the storytelling process informs narrative style lesson planning.

Well-considered lesson stimuli can be as powerful as these openers, enticing children in and sharing intriguing indications of what may be to come. Ben, an undergraduate student teacher, has the following advice, 'Engage using the props and the resources. Plan for something new and different'. Teachers select, reject or transform lesson ideas based upon where the lesson is going: the intended learning outcome or learning objective (see Chapter 4). Often, teachers use published stories to support the structure of lessons and provide the stimuli.

A good story is engaging because it is a kind of dialogue with the reader; the reader questions themselves throughout and predicts where they think the story might be going and, perhaps, is surprised when it takes an unexpected direction. Our aim is for children to be so engaged in a lesson that they too wonder where it is going. The adaptability of the teacher in managing the learning as the series of lessons continues is like the storyteller adding and subtracting different challenges to their quest narrative in light of how their audience (the children) is reacting. And so it progresses the lesson synonymous with the storytelling.

Let the plot begin

Having hooked the class in at the start of the lesson, the narrative then needs to retain their interest and to do this it needs to contain variety and be pitched appropriately. An effective author or storyteller demonstrates control over their narrative by their command of the language. They use different types of sentences for impact, understand the significance of well-chosen repetition, incorporate carefully selected vocabulary or figurative devices and perhaps dialogue to move the action forward. In a similar way, the teacher orchestrates the lesson through precise and dynamic deployment of pedagogic choices, acknowledging the need for changes of pace within the lesson format. Stories are often based on a pattern where characters are faced with a problem or dilemma; the story will reach a climax and culminate in some satisfactory resolution. Following this storyline, we may consider how lesson planning fits within this framework, with a clear planned chronology, enabling the teacher to effectively scaffold learning and encourage independent thought. We might choose to dramatise the story of the lesson, involving the children as 'characters' within the story, setting them a problem or dilemma which they must endeavour to solve or resolve. Teachers' explanations and illustrations can be viewed in themselves as simply 'short stories' within the frame of the main lesson story, using narrative devices to support curriculum delivery (Gudmundsdottir 1991). A lesson may be a 'chapter' in a sequence; there might be 'spin-offs', flashbacks, sequels or even prequels. Lessons can (and should) stretch over several weeks so that the 'readers' (learners) get to know the 'setting' (learning context – in relation to prior learning), the 'characters' (content) and the 'action' (processes) thoroughly. This is summarised in Table 11.1.

When thinking of Harry Potter we might well hear Stephen Fry's voice in our head. For children, when recalling prior learning they may well hear their teachers voice in their head. It is therefore important for us to know how to use

TABLE 11.1 The different forms that narrative can take and how this can influence our planning of the lesson as narrative

Forms of narrative		Lesson planning
Storyboards	Very simple structures which can support learning in the earlier years.	The lesson is mapped into a simple structure with a sequence of key events, activities or lesson phases.
'Chapter' books	The author separates the greater narrative into smaller narratives or chapters. Each needs the others to make complete sense yet the chapters remain an entity in themselves.	The lesson sits within a sequence just as a chapter sits in a book. There are chapters or lessons that precede it and others that follow. Careful progression is planned between the individual chapters or lessons.
Spin-offs	The story might have spin-offs or sequels (think Star Wars Episode IV).	Future lessons might focus upon related topics than run parallel to, follow on from, take a different perspective or explore earlier stages (in greater depth) from a lesson or series of lessons.
Short story	The beauty of the short story is its stand-alone nature.	A lesson can stand alone for a discrete objective, revision or generic skill.
The 'quest'	Where the hero or protagonist has to face a series of challenges	Lessons that position the child as an investigator, problem-solver or explorer and may involve clues, challenges, dilemmas or missing information.

our voice to the best possible effect to tell the story well with clear explanations. Props (or resources) may be developed or collected to support the effective communication of the narrative, to stimulate and to support thinking. To ensure the audience understand the flow of the narrative, sequence of events and make connections, the storyteller will pause during reading and pepper the narrative with questions, prompts and predictions, inviting the listeners to take an active role. Teachers understand the significance of the well-timed pause and plan for a range of questions (explored in Chapter 6) to encourage children to reflect, to assess their comprehension and ability to deduce and infer meaning or indeed to ask questions themselves.

Within a lesson, we need to consider when the children will, for example, be working individually, with partners, or engaging in group work. There needs to be a careful balance of teacher talk and pupil interactivity, all aligned to the learning objective. Just like the characters in a story have different roles and experiences, children in our lessons will have different roles and pathways through the learning. Within the lesson itself, we will need to plan in the moment where we notice that a child is struggling to follow the narrative planned for them and adaptations will need to be made. This is like the editing process in writing – in our head we edit our lesson plan in that moment to more effectively meet the child's learning needs. This is a narrative that is being crafted collaboratively as the class work together with the teacher to construct their learning.

The plot thickens

Some suggest there is a science to storytelling, which enables our brains to become more actively engaged when exploring narrative rather than purely informational-based forms such as bullet-pointed ideas. Essentially, 'a story can put your whole brain to work' (Widrich 2012). This suggests that we, as humans, make use of storytelling, enabling us to relate learning to existing experiences. We make synaptic connections, linking thoughts and ideas from one 'story' (lesson), and experience to the next. This human link to narrative as 'a primary act of mind' (Hardy 1977) reminds us that primary-aged children are familiar with and engage readily with narrative, and that this is clearly linked to their experiences of learning and meaning-making.

> We think in stories. Whenever we encounter new experiences, we use stories we remember, to understand, and to engage in new environments and activities.
>
> (Ryan 2012:1)

In fact, Gudmundsdottir's research shows that many teachers are unaware that they make use of 'curriculum stories' (1991:210) to organise their curriculum and that these stories remain organic in that they are constantly modified and adapted throughout their teaching careers.

Creating engaging lesson narratives, effective use of voice, provision for individual characters, well-used pauses, questioning and interactivity are all important in the lesson as narrative but teacher reflection and flexibility are also essential. After all, a lesson plan is just that a plan and plans can change and alter as needed. Emily, a student teacher, explains: 'You need to know what you will be teaching well enough to be able to teach… but not being over prepared because the lesson might go a completely different way than you prepared for'.

Happily ever after

As the lesson draws to a natural close, there will be the opportunity to reflect on what has been learned and to create a shared understanding of the lesson or narrative. It is important to talk about the story of learning that has occurred. Callum (an undergraduate student teacher) advises that we talk to children about their learning stories, as to 'talk about it afterwards is reflecting on learning'. He suggested that we 'get them to think deeper about what you're trying to teach them'.

For some children, this conclusion will be a satisfying one, and for others it will necessarily provoke other thinking and lead to alternative possibilities. These are the best kinds of narratives: the ones that make us think more. These too are the best kinds of lessons: the ones that promote intellectual curiosity in children, encourage them to ask questions and continue to challenge and make connections. We might also consider whether it is necessary to give away the ending of a lesson. Alternatively, we might choose to pose 'I wonder' questions, enabling children to become co-authors or co-constructors of learning.

For generations, cultures all over the world have passed down stories by word-of-mouth, learning lessons passed from one generation to another. 'Stories have been at the centre of human consciousness for a long time' (Schank 2002:26). Social stories are often used in school to provide opportunities for life lessons, and develop social understanding and relationship skills for young learners who are then able to imagine themselves and others reacting in different social circumstances. Why not apply this across the curriculum to our history, science, maths lessons and beyond, using story as a framework to plan for lessons?

Through effective planning and control of the narrative, the intention is that the learning will be both engaging and easily digested in a form that encourages involvement of the children. Above all, reading or being part of a good story encourages learners to go on reading, to want to turn the page and to read more. A good lesson encourages learners to go on learning, to want to take the next steps in learning and to learn more. Nadim (a postgraduate student teacher) makes the analogy between reading and learning; 'the point of reading a book is to inspire them to do it independently', and surely this independent learning is our intended outcome when we plan and teach a lesson. Gooblar describes this as 'an ingenious trick', that is to encourage narrative learning is to put the children's 'own narrative powers to work for themselves' (Gooblar 2015).

Points to ponder

Where in your lessons do you use engaging 'hooks', strong plots, plot twists and happy ending or provocative conclusions?

Which aspects of this framework will support you in planning for a stand-alone or sequence of lessons?

What type of narratives do you use in your lessons and which might you try to use more?

How might a storyteller approach to using voice, body language and pause support you in teaching engaging and interactive lessons?

How can you ensure that this lesson planning process does not become a 'script' to be followed but rather a narrative to be adapted during teaching?

References

Blackman, M. (2011) *Pig heart boy*. London: Corgi Books.
Bruner, J. (1986) *Actual minds, possible worlds*. Cambridge, MA: Harvard University Press.
Byatt, A. (2000) *On histories and stories*. London: Vintage.
Collins, S. (1993) *Gregor the overlander*. New York: Scholastic.
Department for Education [DfE] (2011) *Teachers' standards: guidance for school leaders, school staff and governing bodies* [online]. Available at: www.gov.uk/government/publications
Egan, K. (1985) Teaching as story-telling: A non-mechanistic approach to planning teaching. *Journal of Curriculum Studies*, 17(4), 397–406.
Gooblar, D. (2015) Narrative in the classroom. *Chronicle Vitae* [online]. Available at: https://chroniclevitae.com/news/1078-narrative-in-the-classroom
Gudmundsdottir, S. (1991) Story-maker, story-teller: narrative structures in curriculum. *Journal of Curriculum Studies*, 23(3), 207–218.

Hardy, B. (1977) Narrative as a primary act of the mind. In: Meek, M., Warlow, A. & Barton, G., eds. *The cool web: The pattern of children's reading*. London: The Bodley Head, 12–23.

Parkin, M. (1998) *Tales for trainers*. London: Kogan Page.

Ryan, P. (2012) *Storytelling is a primary act of the mind* [online]. Available at: https://archive.cilip.org.uk/sites/default/files/i35a%20Storytelling%20is%20a%20primary%20act%20of%20the%20mind%20%20Dr%20Pat%20Ryan.pdf

Schank, R. C. (2002) Every curriculum tells a story. *Tech Directions*, 62(2), 25–29.

Scieszka, J. (1989) *The true story of the three little pigs*. London: Puffin Books.

Sendak, M. (1984) *Where the wild things are*. New York: Harper & Row.

Widrich, L. (2012) *The science of storytelling: Why telling a story is the most powerful way to activate our brains* [online]. Available at: https://lifehacker.com/the-science-of-storytelling-why-telling-a-story-is-the-5965703

12

Planning for children's creativity

Suzanne Gomersall and Catherine Gripton

Introduction

Creativity is a key learning behaviour; it is a way of thinking that supports effective learning. This chapter explores the nature of creativity and why we should plan for it across all curriculum subjects. Essentially, creativity needs to be *planned for* without being *planned out* of the learning experiences we prepare for children in the primary school. This chapter provides three examples of how we, as primary teachers, can effectively plan for children's creativity to increase engagement, extend thinking for all children and ultimately encourage holistic learning and development.

What is creativity and why should we plan for it?

Creativity is thinking and behaving in a certain way by questioning, challenging, making connections, exploring ideas and reflecting (creative thinking). This thinking and behaviour results in purposeful imaginative activity, generating something original and of value (creative doing). Creativity is crucially important, indeed NACCCE (1999:18) argue that it is "...critical to surviving and thriving". It is essential for problem identification and solving as well as higher order thinking and deep understanding. Furthermore, it connects us to others, supports autonomy and is a key part of the development of children as young citizens (CCE 2017, Fisher 2013).

The most common misconception about creativity in primary schools is that it is limited to children having the opportunity for self-expression through certain 'creative subjects' such as art, drama and dance. Creativity is an important element of all curriculum subjects in the primary school requiring us to enable and scaffold children's creativity in all of our teaching. Creativity is therefore a central characteristic of effective learning as emphasised within the Early Years Foundation Stage (EYFS) in England (DfE 2017) where 'creating and thinking critically' is deemed a highly valuable and effective way of learning across the curriculum.

How do we plan for creativity?

Whilst planning for creativity is essential, it can seem counter-intuitive. As teachers, we worry that if we plan too much we will inhibit the children's freedom and stifle their creativity. It can be tempting, particularly as an early career teacher, to instruct and direct the children to aid effective classroom management. In our efforts to plan thoroughly and ensure progress, we can unintentionally limit the possibilities for learning and children's creativity. Possibilities and 'possibility thinking' (Craft 2002) encourage multi-directional thought which opens up pathways, opportunities and choices to children. Children need space and time in order to explore these possibilities: to play and be playful in their thinking (Gripton 2014). They need freedom as well as guidance to make their own choices and form their own connections. Essentially, children need opportunities to take risks. They need teachers who see themselves as facilitators rather than directors of learning so that children can be part-creators in their own creative journeys.

Creative teachers or creative children?

There is the possibility that creative teachers can deprive children of opportunities to be creative and engage in creative thinking for themselves. If it is the teacher who makes the creative connections and thinks of creative ideas then there can be the superficial appearance of creativity in the classroom. However, in this context, it is the teacher and not the learner who is being creative. It is therefore essential when planning for creativity that we avoid doing all the creative thinking *for* the children. The example from Sarah's practice 12.1 demonstrates how children's creativity can be unintentionally undermined by how the activity is introduced and the sharing of success criteria (steps to success or 'what a good one looks like').

Example from practice 12.1: Sarah and the Christmas cards

Sarah was on a teaching practice placement where she was asked to teach a lesson to a class of four- and five-year olds. The class teacher explained to Sarah that this was to be a creative activity intended to support children's learning and development in Expressive Arts and Design (EYFS, DfE 2017). Sarah carefully crafted her lesson plan and prepared all the resources for the children to make Christmas cards. Aware of the need to scaffold children's learning and provide children with clear instructions, Sarah introduced the activity to the class. She showed the children how to create trees using green and brown pipe cleaners with three bends in them. She modelled gluing sequins and sprinkling glitter. She reassured the children that she would help them create bends if needed and showed them her finished card as an example. When the children began making their cards, it did not go as Sarah had anticipated. Sarah explained,

> I tried to encourage the children to think of their own designs but they were mainly worried about getting it 'right' … making it look just like mine! They

kept pushing pipe cleaners in my hands to get me to do it for them. Some children rushed to finish and went off to play as soon as possible. At the end of the day, I put up the cards on a display but they looked like wall paper... 30 cards all the same, one after another, on the wall. I tried to assess how well the children experimented with design but ended up scrapping my assessment grid and assessing fine motor skills instead. I don't think the activity ended up being a creative activity at all really.

Sarah's experience with the Christmas cards demonstrates how crucial it is for teachers to promote *children's* creativity as well as teach creatively themselves. As teachers, we "...challenge, engage and motivate pupils, placing learning within contexts that have relevance for the children" (Desailly 2015:4) but we also do much more than this. We value children's creative thinking by creating a classroom ethos of creativity. Teachers can encourage creativity by embracing all children's ideas (including different and non-standard) and promoting exploration through planning (preparing) for the known and the unknown (what Gripton (2017) calls 'planning for endless possibilities').

What does creativity look like in the primary school?

Within primary schools, there are many different approaches that support teachers to successfully plan for and promote children's creativity, ranging from the National Gallery's 'Take one Picture' to whole curricula based around 'The Big Question'. For the reminder of the chapter, we explore three examples of different approaches to planning for children's creativity in the classrooms. In these examples, teachers planned for children to engage in creative thinking (questioning, challenging, making connections, exploring ideas and reflecting) alongside creative doing (problem identification and problem-solving, purposeful imaginative activity, innovative outcomes) leading to children's deeper understanding.

Increasing children's engagement through immersion in a creative environment

A key benefit of a creative classroom environment is increased engagement and motivation. High levels of engagement, or involvement, are typified by 'intense mental activity' where a child "...is functioning at the very limits of his or her capabilities with an energy that comes from intrinsic sources" (Laevers & Heylen 2003:15). This is much more challenging to achieve where children experience a transmission model of education, where teachers spend large parts of lessons transmitting knowledge and information and the child's role becomes more passive. If children are less engaged, they may become more externally rather than internally motivated leading to a reduction in their level of personal interest, curiosity or enjoyment. Teachers in training can worry about being able to establish a creative environment in a classroom where they are on placement for only a few weeks, but it is possible even within one lesson. In the example from practice 12.2., Lucy's was able to set up a creative learning environment in her writing lesson, which ultimately led to high levels of involvement from the children within her placement class.

Example from practice 12.2: Lucy's immersive writing lesson

With the aim of providing a more creative environment and increasing the children's motivation to write, Lucy took her class into the school hall and began to tell them the story of the 'War of the Roses'. Gradually children took on roles from the story, from Henry Tudor and King Richard III to the fighting soldiers, until all were engaged in the dramatisation. During the battle, Lucy used thought, speech and feeling cards.

What is your character…

… thinking?   … saying?   … feeling?

These prompted the children to answer in character and develop an empathetic perspective, which could be included in their writing. Back in the classroom, the children were given a realistic *Tudor Times* A3 newspaper writing frame and asked to retell the story as if it was a current news event.

> The quality of the final written outcomes, especially from some particular boys who were often reluctant writers, was excellent. They were so excited, motivated and they felt a real purpose to their work that they wrote much more than usual. Most children included quotes from witnesses, soldiers and the new King Henry that were generated through the re-enactment, as well as emotive phrases, which I feel would have certainly been missing had the children not had the opportunity to immerse themselves in the battlefield environment, said Lucy.

Using problem-solving to develop all children's higher order thinking

It is important for all children to think creatively as a higher order thinking skill. As teachers, it can seem challenging to find a way of developing the thinking skills of *all* children and solve problems whilst meeting the needs of every individual child. With this in mind, Wallace and Adams (Wallace 2000) created the 'Thinking Actively in a Social Context' (T.A.S.C.) framework which provides a structure for the different stages of the thinking process which children use to solve a problem including reflecting upon their own learning. This opportunity to reflect is vital if learners are to consolidate new learning and transfer this to a range of contexts and areas of curriculum. The example from Peter's practice 12.3 illustrates how this approach can encourage all children to use higher order thinking skills whilst, at the same time, working within all key elements of creativity.

Example from Practice 12.3: Peter and the T.A.S.C. approach

Peter's art lessons for his Tudor topic would normally involve the children painting a portrait of one of the Tudor kings or queens, providing the opportunity for a range of skills and techniques to be taught and then applied. This year, Peter wanted to introduce elements of choice and open-endedness and enable the children to be part-creators in their own creative journeys so he set the children a problem: 'To create a piece of artwork to depict a Tudor king or queen for display in a class art gallery'. Consequently, the children were able to discuss and generate many ways to depict the kings and queens using a wide range of media. Peter selected four possible outcomes from the children's ideas: clay, paint, drawing and Lego.

> If I had limited the outcomes to my own selection, Lego would not have been considered. This way, the learning context is authentic for the children as they understood the medium of Lego, as many played with it at home. The concept of a 3D representation hadn't crossed my mind when I planned this!

To enable the children to make an informed choice from the four options, Peter taught all the children the art skills required (shading and tone, shaping and joining clay and use of contrast in colour) and historical enquiry skills (selecting and evaluating evidence) in order to research their king or queen and depict them with historical accuracy.

> I was amazed by the children's thinking skills at all stages of the process, as well as how much they valued their work and were able to reflect upon how they got there. The children showed a high level of involvement as they were able to choose their medium and knew that their work was going to be viewed and appraised in a class 'Art Gallery' at the end of term. The Lego group had to quickly develop their perseverance and problem-solving skills as it soon became clear that there were not enough of the right Lego bricks to build a 3-D statue so, through discussion, they quickly adapted and made two dimensional representations which was reflected upon in the children's evaluations, said Peter.

Children making meaningful connections: cross-curricular or holistic learning?

Making connections between subjects can be a key way to support children's creative thinking. However, we can go a step further than cross-curricular teaching to think about planning for children's holistic learning. Holistic learning is more than making connections across subjects but is about developing the whole child including academic, social and emotional learning as well as their learning dispositions or habits (their learning skills, approaches or behaviours). In planning for children's holistic learning, we aim for a broad and balanced curriculum that retains the specific nature of each subject whilst supporting the children to learn in a connected rather than separated way. However, if subject clarity and integrity is sacrificed, a rainbow curriculum of subjects is in danger of becoming a single 'topic' of "mucky brown paint" where the uniqueness of each subject is lost (Fox-Turnbull 2012:79). If subjects are taught together effectively they work alongside and enhance each other and therefore provide meaningful learning experiences for children.

Example from practice 12.4: Anna's pop-up book project

Anna saw the opportunity to make meaningful connections between learning about the human body in science, non-fiction texts in English and mechanisms in design and technology. She designed a small project where her class (aged 9–10 years old) created pop-up books about the human body for children (aged 5–6 years old) in their school.

Anna was astounded by the children's engagement and learning, not just in these three specific curriculum areas but in other ways too. Anna reported,

> The children were taught all of these subject areas separately, but through the project, the learning was combined and all the children created pop up books and thoroughly enjoyed having the opportunity to share and explain their products to the younger children.

She continued,

> …certain children really shone during this project. One child, for example, who often struggled with behaviour at school showed real motivation and perseverance to complete their book; another child who rarely spoke in class, was in full flow describing their book to another child in the class – a real magical moment to witness.

In Anna's example from practice 12.4, she supported children to meet curriculum expectations in three subject areas by enhancing their motivation and involvement, providing meaningful connections between authentic subject learning and also their wider holistic development. Children developed more effective learning habits, displaying greater perseverance and some developed socially with enhanced confidence. Cross-curricular and holistic learning experiences can also support depth of learning with children constructing conceptual understanding as they make connections. This idea of developing deeper understanding through making connections is evident within teaching for mastery approaches in mathematics and also in project-based curriculum approaches such as is used in the educational settings of Reggio Emilia in Italy. Projects encourage conceptual understanding through a focus upon '-ness'. So, for example, a project on 'rivers' would consider 'river-ness' which would include a conceptual understanding of essentially what a river is and what it is not. This approach develops depth of understanding in terms of how a river is different to a lake, a puddle or a canal.

Conclusion

Through immersion in a creative environment, solving problems and making meaningful connections children's creativity can thrive. This requires teachers to demonstrate personal qualities such as risk-taking and curiosity as well as effective pedagogy within an ethos of creativity. Children need to have the opportunity for choice, independence, risk and freedom. Teachers sometimes report a tension between creativity and pressure to ensure children meet educational standards. Perhaps, we could look at this another way. Perhaps creativity is the way for children to achieve the highest standards through high levels of involvement, higher order thinking and deep conceptual understanding. In planning any lesson or sequence of lessons, we need to consider what and where the opportunities are for:

- Involving the children in the planning
- Enhancing the learning in specific subject areas by making meaningful connections across subjects
- The children to be imaginative (generating new ideas, being intuitive, making connections, communicating in interesting or varied ways)
- Enquiry-based learning and problem-solving (exploring, wondering, posing questions and challenging assumptions)
- Developing children's values and learning behaviours or dispositions (for example, inquisitiveness, persistence, imagination, collaboration and discipline as suggested by Lucas, Claxton & Spencer 2013)
- Extending and developing ideas further (adapting, making connections, evaluation, refining and improving)

As we have argued in this chapter, creativity can enable these for children. In this sense, planning for creativity is really just planning for effective teaching (Jeffrey & Craft 2001) as 'the best education has creativity at its heart' (Creativity Culture Education 2017).

Points to ponder

Careful consideration of the possible pathways or directions that learning may take enables teachers to plan for creative possibilities in learning. Before designing specific lessons, teachers can look for the opportunities for children's creativity at an early stage in the planning process. One way would be to consider a range of prompts in planning, such those suggested in Figure 12.1. Suggest this paragraph moves to after the questions and there is a line space between the paragraph and the questions.

How can children be more involved in planning the learning opportunities that they engage with (as a class group and as an individual making choices about how they will learn)?

How can we enhance learning through supporting children to make meaningful connections across subjects yet ensure that the subject-specific learning is not muddied or lost?

How do we create a learning environment where children's creativity is fostered and every child can develop creative dispositions such as inquisitiveness, persistence, imagination, collaboration and discipline?

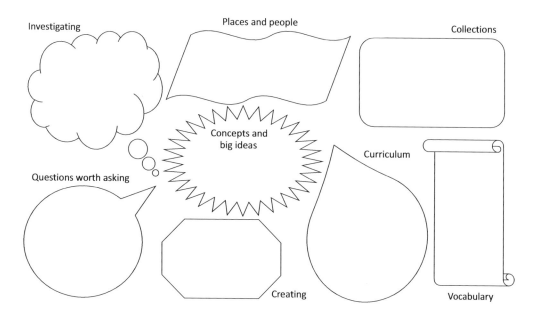

Investigating

Places and people

Collections

Concepts and big ideas

Questions worth asking

Curriculum

Creating

Vocabulary

FIGURE 12.1 Possible prompts for planning for children's creativity.

References

Craft, A. (2002) *Creativity and early years education: A lifewide foundation.* London: Continuum.

Creativity Culture Education. (2017) *What we believe* [online]. Available at: www.creativitycultu-reeducation.org. Accessed on 13 Oct 2017.

Department for Education (DfE), (2017) *Statutory framework for the early years foundation stage: Setting the standards for learning, development and care for children from birth to five.* London: Department for Education.

Desailly, J. (2015) *Creativity in the primary classroom.* 2nd Ed. London: Sage.

Fisher, R. (2013) What is creativity? In: Fisher, R. & Williams, M., eds., *Unlocking creativity: Teaching across the curriculum.* Oxon: Routledge, 2013, 6–20.

Fox-Turnbull, W. (2012) Learning in technology. In: Williams, J., ed., *Technology education for teachers.* Rotterdam: Sense Publishers, 2012, 55–92.

Gripton, C. (2014) Playing with thinking. In: Woods, A., ed., *The characteristics of effective learning: Creating and capturing the possibilities in the early years,* Oxon: Routledge, 2014, 71–86.

Gripton, C. (2017) Planning for endless possibilities. In: Woods, A., ed., *Child-initiated play and learning: Planning for possibilities in the early years,* 2nd ed. London: David Fulton, 2017, 8–22.

Jeffrey, B. & Craft, A. (2001) The universalization of creativity. In: Craft, A., Jeffrey, B. & Leibling, M., eds., *Creativity in education.* Continuum: London, 2001, 1–16.

Laevers, F. & Heylen, L., eds., (2003) *Involvement of children and teaching style: Insights from an international study on experiential education.* Leuven: Leuven University Press

Lucas, B., Claxton, G. & Spencer, E. (2013) *Progression in student creativity in school: First steps towards new forms of formative assessments,* OECD education working papers, No. 86. Paris: Organisation for Economic Co-operation and Development.

National Advisory Committee on Creative and Cultural Education [NACCCE]. (1999) *All our futures: Creativity, culture and education.* London: Department for Education and Employment.

Wallace, B. (2000) Teaching thinking and problem-solving skills. *Educating Able Children,* 4, 20–24.

13

Promoting a positive climate for learning

Helen Fielding, Eleanor Power and Nick Page

Introduction

A climate for learning can be described as an atmosphere or environment that is positive, respectful and supportive so that all children learn effectively. This positive classroom ethos, which a teacher seeks to promote, is integral to the success of lessons and so needs to be deliberately cultivated (planned for). Ways of promoting a positive climate for learning are explored within this chapter.

We, as teachers, have a critical role in creating this positive climate, modelling the learning behaviours we are seeking to promote. Ideally, we are seeking to create a climate where all children feel comfortable so that they are able to participate and contribute fully, including through the asking and answering of questions. Offering a suitable level of challenge for all within the class is a key element of the promotion of a positive climate for learning. Many overarching decisions that we make as teachers are based on the ethos of the school and our personal educational philosophy. These decisions are further shaped by curriculum demands, subject knowledge and knowledge of the children. All these decisions affect the climate for learning.

When planning lessons, we are seeking to engage children across a wide range of subjects and promote interest and excitement to learn, regardless of our own personal preferences and curricular strengths. We are aiming to provide each child with the opportunity to become actively involved and independent within the lesson. As teachers, we are seeking to create a climate of learning where children feel curious and want to know more or explore in further depth. One aspect of this is the promotion of intellectual curiosity.

Promoting intellectual curiosity

What do we mean by intellectual curiosity? Curiosity has led to incredible steps forwards. Dann (2013) points out the significance of NASA naming the Mars rover 'Curiosity', reflecting how curiosity propels us towards important new understandings. We should similarly let curiosity 'rove unmanned' through our classrooms

(Dann 2013:558), following children's natural inquisitiveness to support significant new learning for children. Intellectual curiosity is fundamental for learning. Dewey (1933) explains that we need to harness our natural curiosity to avoid becoming overwhelmed by the sheer volume (or tsunami) of knowledge at our fingertips; this is even more the case with unlimited resources available with a simple tap of the keys of a computer. We can define this intellectual curiosity as the joy of or thirst for learning that leads to the asking of questions and encompasses the desire to pursue different avenues of thought: the pursuit of the 'unknown unknowns'.

The question for us as teachers is therefore how we promote and harness the child's innate curiosity within a positive climate for learning which enables them to take ownership of the learning process.

Some curricula and approaches guide teachers to teach curiosity explicitly. In England, all teachers are required to promote a 'love of learning' (DfE 2011:11) and provide 'a sense of enjoyment and curiosity' about mathematics (DfE 2013:99), although how this is achieved is up to the individual teacher. In contrast, the Te Whariki early years curriculum in New Zealand (2017:23) identifies key learning dispositions which are regarded as being valuable in developing life-long learners. It states that 'the disposition to be curious involves having the inclination and skills to inquire into and puzzle over ideas and events'. Our challenge is to promote development of these inquiry skills alongside providing opportunities and stimuli that children will be curious about and which allow them to apply these skills.

Developing curiosity in children involves the conscious promotion of risk-taking which requires confidence from the teacher: something that can be difficult in the initial years of being responsible for a class. It is however important, and by modelling a risk-taking approach, we aim to generate the same approach in the children. It is therefore crucial for us, as teachers, to put a 'toe in the water' and try taking risks in our practice. This can begin by choosing interesting, alternative or unexpected stimuli for learning. The curiosity and questions of the children can be focused and steered by engaging them through initial hooks to lessons and/or topics (see chapter 11). Some caution is needed as this can be a potential pitfall for the teacher during the planning process. Interesting 'activities' can overtake the learning focus, and the 'learning' can become lost. The role of the teacher is that of a route finder, helping to chart a way through to the learning destination using intellectual curiosity as the compass (rather than the destination). Ostroff, in *Cultivating Curiosity*, points out the teacher role in harnessing and channelling children's curiosity. She claims that the teacher needs to provide support for learning alongside encouraging children's curiosity when she states that 'playful curiosity plus scaffolding can transform into learning' (2016:1). To enable this transformation of curiosity into learning, there is a required shift in our perspectives from being a 'teacher' to modelling being a 'teacher learner' and by asking our own questions and sharing our own learning, charting explicitly where we were led by our own curiosity.

In planning, it comes back to the formulation of a probing and well thought through question, perhaps enhanced with a morsel of intriguing information to stimulate the interest. Some schools use the KWL (Ogle 1986) approach, shown in Table 13.1, as a scaffold to allow children to frame the questions that they want answered within a specific theme. Claxton (2019) argues that it is crucial that teachers create an environment where children are encouraged to have a sense of entitlement that they have a right

TABLE 13.1 The KWL approach

K – what we know already	W – what we want to learn	L – what we have learned
This is where either an individual child writes what they know or a class version is created where the teacher collates the shared knowledge.	The children write down questions about what they want to find out. These can be used to guide the direction the learning takes.	At the end of a topic, the children identify key elements of what they have learned.

(Adapted from Ogle 1986).

to be curious, ask questions and to discuss. This has implications for teachers' subject knowledge and how we respond to those questions when we are ourselves unsure of the answer. Learning is iterative in this respect as there is a need for teachers to model active learning and our own curiosity in our responses to the children.

Challenges in learning – mistakes and misconceptions

Children may face difficulties and challenges in any subject across the curriculum therefore it is particularly important to build a climate where children feel confident and comfortable to minimise the effects of these difficulties. As a beginning teacher, it is vital to have good personal subject knowledge of the topic being taught and an understanding of the possible misconceptions the children may hold. In mathematics lessons, for example, where responses to questions can sometimes be considered either right or wrong, children often feel that their incorrect answers will be more evident to their peers. Misconceptions can be planned for within a lesson, so possible pitfalls are considered, and approaches can be modelled to avoid promoting these further. However, some misconceptions are inevitable. The teacher's approach and attitude when misconceptions or errors arise can be crucial in how the child is able to proceed and feel able to cope with the difficulty. We are seeking to build the children's confidence and avoid undermining their belief in themselves as learners.

Swan suggests that frequently, a 'misconception' is not wrong thinking but is a concept in embryo or a local generalisation that the pupil has made. It may in fact be a natural stage of development (2001:154). If we view misconceptions as an essential step within learning they can be viewed as helpful and possibly even necessary. We can therefore seek to promote the approach that "We learn from our mistakes". Then we can avoid diminishing children's self-confidence and offer the opportunity to build on the difficulties encountered. For example, occasionally a child will declare themselves "stuck" or state that they "don't get it". The teacher could perhaps consider asking them to explain what they have achieved so far and identify at which point they have ceased to understand, or whether they can explain how this question differs from the last one. This may be the time when we realise that many children have reached the same point and that what is needed is a mini-plenary to support everyone.

The opportunity to share and discuss aspects of learning which are proving difficult is always valuable, but needs practice from both the teacher and the children. Talking mathematics, for example, is not something that may come easily initially but the establishment of a sharing and listening environment will support many learners within the class. An agreed class signal which shows the speaker that they are in agreement and were thinking the same thing can be very reassuring and build the confidence of the child who is offering the explanation. Also practising your own explanations, as the teacher, to share mathematical thinking, will offer a useful model for the children to emulate. The choice of teacher language can be crucial here, whilst we are sometimes acknowledging that this element of the work is proving tricky, we do not want to imply that it is difficult and discourage the child from persisting.

Developing resilience

There are many definitions of resilience including the ability to bounce back or cope, learn and thrive following change, difficulties, challenges or adversity (Johnson 2008, Joslyn 2016). Building a child's resilience is an important part of the school's ethos and its well-being approach and does not only relate to academic aspects but also to the social and emotional elements of school life and beyond.

Everyone, within their primary school days, has at some point found some elements within a subject problematic, and developing a child's inclination to persist and show resilience is what will make a difference when they next face a similar difficulty. Within our planning, we may consider how to support the building of academic resilience, by providing the opportunity to solve problems. This problem-solving approach can offer children the chance to make decisions about how to proceed with a task and explore different possibilities within a supported setting. Allowing the freedom to make decisions can possibly be more important than the outcome and can give a child the chance to persist and be resilient in a shared working group. This opportunity to solve problems also provides a range of transferable skills as well as exploring aspects of the curriculum in more depth. Communication and reasoning skills can be built through the posing of suitable problems in any subject, whether establishing spelling rules or designing a sandwich.

We, as teachers, can develop this in our children by integrating tentative language into our teaching. By using phrases such as 'I don't know, let's find out…', 'I wonder what would happen if…', 'Shall we try…', 'Let's see if this works…', children see that if their teacher doesn't always know the answers but is at ease with it, they will come to see uncertainty as a positive rather than a negative.

The use of 'Low Threshold, High Ceiling' problems, for example, in mathematics (discussed briefly in Chapter 4) suggests an approach where problems are selected for their initial accessibility. The majority of the children can begin to explore in a meaningful way and can be successful on a range of levels. Yet, the problem additionally offers a range of possibilities and greater levels of challenge to allow children the opportunity to be independent and explore further. This is a model worth considering in other subjects.

Perceptions of challenge

What would life be like if learning was a predictable, linear process, where teaching inputs were immediately in direct proportion with learning outcomes? Children can sometimes see this as the ideal standard. They can feel that they should understand something fully and immediately, and if they fall short of this ideal, they can see themselves as failing in some way. Learning is rarely simple and linear. Learning takes time, and we may well make mistakes or fail repeatedly before we truly master something. When learning to ride a bike, falling off the bike is not failing, it is a necessary part of the process of learning to ride. We have to be prepared to fall off that bike and get back on again multiple times in order to reach our goal. Helping children understand this process of learning is vital for their self-esteem and resilience. In example from practice 13.1, we learn about how Ruth and Ali develop and sustain their approach to achieving this in their Nottinghamshire school.

Example from practice 13.1: Building perseverance

Ruth Spencer and Ali Bell from Lowe's Wong Anglican Methodist Junior School, Southwell, explained how they developing a whole school approach to building learner perseverance.

As a school, we were introduced to James Nottingham's 'learning pit' during a professional development session (Nottingham 2017). We immediately saw the potential benefits for our children. We were struggling with how children seemed to give up easily when they first found something difficult. They perhaps believed that because they couldn't do something straight away, they would never be able to master it. We have a lot of high achieving children in our school, and it can be these 'rapid graspers' who appear to be hit hardest by not being able to do something. They are used to instant success and achieving without maximum effort. They are not always used to finding things hard, being 'stuck' or failing. They are mostly children for whom learning can often be a predictable, linear process. Therefore, when they do meet something they do not understand, they can easily become disheartened and they do not know how to deal with this perceived failure. Dweck states, 'Many of the most confident individuals do not want their intelligence too stringently tested, and their high confidence is all too quickly shaken when they are confronted with difficulty' (2002:2), and this was true for our children. The learning pit represents an acceptance that learning is hard and it embraces the idea that failure is a vital part of learning, reminding us what the learning process is like.

We start with a concept that the children have some understanding of. When they find something difficult, their understanding of the concept is challenged or they don't understand – they go into 'the pit'. This cognitive conflict in the minds of the children leads to them beginning to construct meaning for themselves as they work their way out of the pit. Previously, children may have given up, however, 'the pit' has given us a vital concept for showing children that this is how learning works: you will fail, you will make mistakes and you will be confused and not understand. In our school, children can go and put their name on 'the pit' displays in their classroom to acknowledge their struggle. To put themselves in 'the pit' shows they understand that it is alright to find something hard but that it is not okay to give in and wallow in that feeling of helplessness. Indeed, it's good to be in the pit: now the real learning starts, it can even be enjoyable if you let it!

The children are taught about how they can help themselves get out of 'the pit'. Perhaps they need to re-read the question, or ask a friend for help, try out new strategies or look for clues on the display boards. They know that you are never completely on your own in 'the pit' but they are not simply fed the answers, they must solve the problems for themselves. As teachers we know that if we always hold the children's hands and never let them fall, slip or tumble into 'the pit' then they will never have to truly think for themselves. The successes would not be their own, and they would never learn to fully appreciate the 'Eureka' moment that solving a problem for yourself brings.

Periodically during the school year, we have 'pit days' where we reintroduce the 'learning pit' idea to the children. We give them carefully planned activities that practise the skills of resilience, and encourage problem-solving and the dialogue around cooperation and sharing ideas. We ensure that we celebrate learning from our mistakes. The idea is also regularly discussed in assemblies. For example, the children were introduced to 'famous failures', such as Steve Jobs or James Dyson, to show that nothing great was ever achieved without effort and that perseverance is important even in the face of failure. This approach is what we want from our children – to fully believe that with effort, they can achieve. When things are difficult, they just haven't quite mastered it 'yet', but with appropriate effort, they will.

For a positive learning climate in the classroom, the children must feel able to attempt a challenge without worrying about the consequences of not succeeding. A fear of failure puts the handbrake on any desire to attempt things new or unfamiliar. Dweck (2007) discusses the impact that learner mindset has on this, particularly the learner's understanding of where intelligence comes from. Where a child's perception is that intellectual ability is something that one is born with and cannot change (a 'fixed mindset') then they believe intelligence to be the key factor in being successful as a learner. They may feel that any mistake reflects negatively on their own capability, and see their mistakes as showing that perhaps they are less intelligent. In order to avoid their self-esteem being undermined, a child may actively avoid challenge in certain subjects or situations and avoid taking risks, showing aspects of a fixed mindset. In contrast, a child viewing intellectual ability as something which can develop through the effort and application of specific strategies to particular problems shows a 'growth mindset'. They will want to seek out challenge in order to develop their intellectual ability further.

So how can we as teachers help children to develop a growth mindset? First, a teacher needs to recognise when a fixed mindset feeling or situation occurs and avoid perpetuating this by enabling children to feel that they have a choice. Teachers can model a growth mindset 'voice' and support children to reflect on their learning through encouragement when situations are proving taxing. In using a growth mindset voice, we might use sentences such as "The point isn't to get it all right straight away, but to develop your understanding step by step. What shall we try next?". If a child expresses that they are 'not a maths person' or say they are 'no good at science' then we can add "yet" to the end of the sentence (as the teachers do in the example from practice). This helps the child to appreciate there is the possibility of change and growth. Teachers can encourage children to adopt a growth mindset approach so a child feels they have the choice to:

- Take on a challenge wholeheartedly
- Learn from setbacks and try again
- Listen to constructive feedback and act on it

TABLE 13.2 Different approaches to support a positive climate and disposition for learning

The 5R's (Guy Claxton)	These are comprised of resilience, resourcefulness, remembering, reflectiveness and responsiveness. By developing these skills, the teacher aims to equip pupils with what they need to become independent learners.
'Ask three before me'	This is often represented as a poster in the classroom and directs children to pursue three avenues of investigation in answering a question before going to the teacher, thereby freeing up the teacher to focus their input according to where they have identified a need. In some cases, the strategy is known as 'three before me' (3B4ME) or 'three Bs': brain, book and buddy (asking the children to pause and think, to research or to ask another child).
Traffic lights/RAG rating	Using red, amber and green cards, children indicate whether they need support. The requirement to put a hand up and ask for help is therefore avoided.
Phone a friend	This notion is borrowed from the 'Who Wants to be a Millionaire' television programme and is intended to build a sense of cooperation where children can be supported by others when they find themselves unable to answer a question.

As teachers we need to actively support children to develop a positive attitude to challenges and making mistakes. A few possible approaches are presented in Table 13.2. Resnick (2007), co-creator of the Scratch programming language, places great importance on children learning through a process of imagining, creating, playing, sharing and reflecting. The reflection is crucial as it is where children are identifying their own errors and suggesting improvements for themselves. Rather than avoiding mistakes, the children are actively seeking them in order to correct them. When Resnick asked children for tips they would give other children when using new technologies, their suggestions included, *'Don't be afraid to experiment,'* and *'Lots of things can go wrong, stick with it.'*

These children seemed to embrace uncertainty, welcoming the possibilities that might arise by doing so. When presented with technological tools that were new to them, their willingness to try something new, regardless of whether they knew it would work or not, resulted in coming up with original and exciting ways of using them by themselves. Resnick's work has influenced the design of the National Curriculum for Computing in England (DfE 2013) and the related guidance on Computational Thinking (Csizmadia et al. 2015), which makes explicit reference to concepts and approaches which encourage a positive approach to challenge:

- Debugging – Mistakes will happen, so learn to identify and rectify them
- Evaluation – Actively seek out what works and what does not
- Tinkering – Play around with the tools and find out what happens
- Perseverance – Challenges can be overcome by drawing on what you have learned.

Being comfortable with uncertainty is, it would seem, something to be encouraged in our classrooms. Claxton (2007:2) goes so far as to say that 'tolerance for hazy or non-articulate ways of knowing is essential to learning' as learning 'weaves in and out of periods of confusion and ambiguity'. Problem-solving activities across the curriculum can support children to develop an openness to challenges and experimentation, and help children to feel comfortable with some periods of uncertainty as a normal part of learning.

Conclusion

In this chapter we have considered some of the ways teachers promote a positive climate for learning. The teacher has an essential role within this; as a consideration at the planning stage for a lesson or sequence, but also as an integral part of a teacher's approach to the whole curriculum and part of the class ethos. A positive learning climate is inextricably linked with all elements of teaching. Our actions and beliefs shape children's responses, for example, having and sharing high expectations of all children helps promote a positive learning climate. As teachers, we aim to model the learning behaviours we are seeking to promote by showing intellectual curiosity, being active problem-solvers, demonstrating resilience and welcoming challenge.

Points to ponder

Everyone experiences struggle and moments where learning has proved difficult. How can we support children to expect to experience this and what to do when it is happening for them?

What are the best approaches for teachers to take when specific learning is proving difficult for a child? What will help the child succeed and feel more confident?

What ways of thinking act as a blockage to overcoming difficulty? How can these be addressed?

Consider approaches for building confidence that have you observed in the classroom.

How can we implement or adapt approaches for building learner confidence and integrate them into our teaching to support the learning climate?

What approaches can teachers use to promote independence?

Which of the approaches in Table 13.2 are most appropriate for older/younger children or a particular school ethos or setting? How do they map to the educational philosophies of individual teachers?

References

Claxton, G. (2007) Expanding young people's capacity to learn. *British Journal of Educational Studies*, 55(2), 115–134.

Claxton, G. (2019) *Building learning power* [online]. Available at: www.buildinglearningpower.com

Csizmadia, A., Curzon, P., Dorling, M., Humphreys, S., Ng, T., Selby, C., & Woollard, J. (2015). *Computational thinking: A guide for teachers*. Swindon: Computing at School.

Dann, R. (2013) Be curious: Understanding 'curiosity' in contemporary curriculum policy and practice. *Education 3–13*, 41(6), 557–561.

Department for Education [DfE]. (2011) *Teachers' standards: Guidance for school leaders, school staff and governing bodies* [online]. Available at: www.gov.uk/government/publications/teachers-standards

Department for Education [DfE]. (2013) *National curriculum for England [online].* Available at: www.gov.uk/government/collections/national-curriculum

Dewey, J. (1933) *How we think.* Boston: Houghton Mifflin.

Dweck, C. (2002) *Self-theories: Their role in motivation, personality and development.* London: Psychology Press.

Dweck, C. (2007) Boosting achievement with messages that motivate. *Education Canada,* 47(2), 6–10.

Johnson, B. (2008) Teacher–student relationships which promote resilience at school: A micro-level analysis of student's views. *Journal of Guidance and Counselling,* 36(4), 385–398.

Joslyn, E. (2016) *Resilience in childhood: Perspectives, promise and practice.* London: Palgrave.

Nottingham, J. (2017) *The learning challenge: How to guide your students through the learning pit to achieve deeper understanding.* London: Sage.

Ogle, D. M. (1986) K-W-L: A teaching model that develops active reading of expository text. *Reading Teacher,* 39(6), 564–570.

Ostroff, W. L. (2016) *Cultivating curiosity in K-12 classrooms.* Alexandria: ASCD.

Resnick, M. (2007) *All I really need to know (about creative thinking) I learned (by studying how children learn) in Kindergarten* [online]. Available at: https://web.media.mit.edu/~mres/papers/kindergarten-learning-approach.pdf

Swan, M. (2001) Dealing with misconceptions in mathematics. In: Gates, P. ed. *Issues in teaching mathematics.* London: Routledge, 147–165.

Index

Note: **Bold** page numbers refer to tables; *Italic* page numbers refer to figures.